STOCK TRADING STRATEGIES

3 Manuscripts: Stock Trading, Day Trading and Options Trading for Beginners

BY SAM SUTTON

Table of Contents

Stock Trading

The Beginner's Guide to Turning the Stock Market into Your Personal ATM

By Sam Sutton

Introduction

So, you want to learn a bit about the Stock Market and how to make some extra money through it. No problem. You've downloaded the right book. You can now officially check off the first item on your "to do" list -- given that item is "download the best and most comprehensive guide to the stock market for beginner's."

But all joking aside, the stock market is a dangerous game to play. Yes, it's true that trading stocks is a method with which someone may make a large amount of money, but the exact opposite is also true: There's a decent chance that someone may lose money as well. Trading stocks on the stock market is a sort of gamble at time, you'll be playing with fire. You'll be playing with fire while gambling. It's not a great combination.

But, with the tips and guidance provided in this book, you can minimize your chance at burning yourself -- or, in a more literal sense, losing money.

It won't be easy. Like all money-making ventures, working with the stock market requires practice, skill, patience, a little bit of luck, and a good amount of know-how. It's pretty difficult to write a book about "how to get luckier," so these pages are filled with tips and tricks to help you learn and practice the basics, developing the proper skills, and understanding the basic know-how associated with trading stocks.

Chapter 1: Starting Out in the Stock Market

Chances are, if you're new at trying something-- everything from tying your shoes to performing surgery. Like everything else you could possibly do, trading stocks take practice. You won't be good right away and that's perfectly acceptable.

That being said, mistakes are to be expected, but the mistakes are with your money. You have to be cautious with how quickly you jump into the stock market ocean; too quickly and you have a high chance to lose a lot of your well-earned money, too quickly and you may lose your chance to buy the perfect stock at the perfect price.

There are tons of variables that go into buying, selling, and trading stocks that many people don't consider when they first enter into the game. Luckily, you were smart enough to download this book before diving in head first.

The first chapter covers the basics that everyone needs to know when they first enter the stock market. The sections are divided up into commonly asked questions to better help you, the reader, find the answers or information you're looking for.

First thing's first...

What are Stocks?

The companies offer up little bits of ownership (called stocks) to anyone who wants to buy them. When someone buys stocks, the company is then allowed to use that money to do with as they please (usually this money goes to products, or property, or other assets the company needs to grow).

Two basic things happen when someone invests in a company and buys stock:

1. The buyer legally owns a small portion of the company
    a. Usually, a single stock is worth very, very little of the company's overall ownership.
    b. Rather than "owning some of a company," the buyer owns stocks in said company.
2. The company or business gains money from the sale to use to improve their company.

What Exactly is the Stock Market?

The stock market is a general term used to define a place (either a physical location, or a digital server) where stocks are sold, bought, and traded. Where many first time investors get confused in the terminology involved.

For example:

- An investor is a person that buys stock in one or multiple companies.
- A stock <u>market</u> is a term used to describe anywhere that deals with stocks and the trading of stocks.
    - This term is often used when teaching individuals about trading stock at a stock exchange, but can also be used to describe the entire process of trading stocks.
- A stock <u>exchange</u>, on the other hand, is a specific location that deals in the buying, selling, and trading of companies' stocks.

To help you keep these terms straight in your head, think about when you go to get pizza for dinner. If you say "I'm going to get pizza for dinner," it allows people to know what you're doing, but doesn't tell them the details. Anyone listening in understands that you're going to get a pizza from somewhere. Saying "I'm going to get pizza for dinner" is equivalent to the stock market. It's a general statement that tells people basically what you're doing in a nutshell.

If you were to say "I'm going to Domino's to pick up a pizza," you're telling anyone that's listening what you are doing and where. Domino's Pizza is the stock exchange you choose to use.

Just remember: The <u>stock market is general</u>, the <u>stock exchange is specific</u>.

The stock market as a whole allows companies to put themselves out there to the public. This creates a sort of mutually beneficial (or mutually destructive) relationship between the company and its investors.

What is a Stock Exchange Then?

Stock exchanges are the individual places that a person may buy, sell, or trade stocks. While the term "Stock Market" refers to the business, as it were, of buying, selling, and trading stocks, the exchanges that make up the stock market are the veritable storefronts of the stock trading world.

Some stock exchanges are common in media such as film and television shows to show the hussle and bussle associated with the business world. The most commonly named stock exchange is the New York Stock Exchange (also known as NYSE or "The Big Board"). The New York Stock Exchange is the largest stock exchange in the world and more than

1.5 billion dollars can be bought, sold, and traded through the New York Stock Exchange daily. Whenever a movie shows crowds of men and women in suits yelling and waving papers around in a room full of television monitors, they are usually depicting this specific stock exchange.

While a large percentage of the larger stock exchanges (the New York Stock Exchange being a prime example) are stressful and fast-paced and a bit over the top for anyone who hasn't made a living out of trading stocks, there are alternatives for any person just wanting to dip their big toe, so to speak.

A relatively recent form of stock exchanges are the online stock exchanges, which are any held through a website or internet domain. They often times require a subscription fee to use their services, but offer a much more relaxed environment for anyone just starting out.

Are there risks involved with online stock exchanges? Of course there are. There is still that looming risk of losing money through poor decisions or plain old bad luck, but there isn't the stress and fast moving atmosphere most people associate with buying, selling, and trading stocks.

In either case (whether you prefer to go into a physical location to trade stocks, or decide to stay home and do it on the computer), there are tons upon tons of options to choose from. Each stock exchange functions the same, more or less, with a few tweaks to rules, subscriptions, and other details here and there, so if you can learn to use one, you probably will do alright with the others.

In terms of physical location stock exchanges, it depends on where you live or work. You'll have to do some research regarding the surrounding areas to see what is available to you. You can also find a <u>stockbroker</u>.

A stockbroker is someone you pay to buy and sell stocks for you. And don't worry, he or she will have your best interests at heart because, after all, the more you make, the more he or she makes in the process.

If you would rather dive into the world of online stock exchange, there are still plenty of choices to choose from, and chances are you've seen a commercial for one or two over the last few years.

Commonly used and popular online stock brokerages include:

- Scottrade
- Tradestation
- Etrade
- Ameritrade

- And others.

You'll have to look more into the details of each individual brokerage to find one that suits your needs best (never just go with the first one you happen upon, always compare).

How Does Someone Make Money Buying and Selling Stocks?

The entire purpose of buying, selling, and trading stocks is to make money. Sure, a lot of people do it as a hobby in their free time (or as a full-fledged career), but no one wants to lose money on the stock market.

With that goal in mind, there are two possible ways to make money buying, selling, and trading stocks on the stock market:

1. Buy Low Priced Stocks Then Sell Them When They Go Up in Price.

Buying and selling stocks when the price is right is a good way to gain or lose a chunk of your money in an instant. This is the strategy that introduced the idea of "buy low, sell high" which you may have heard once or twice in your lifetime.

Buying stocks with a low price point (usually

companies that are just starting out, or companies that aren't doing so well) will allow you to buy more at a lower price and hold onto them until their price goes up. Once the stocks' prices have increased to an amount you're happy with, you can sell them on the exchange. Because of the rise in price, your selling them for more than you originally bought them for.

Here's a trick that many people don't consider in the long run: If you buy a lot of stocks at a low price (maybe even several hundred or thousand) and the price only goes up a few dollars, you have to remember that the price of each and every stock you bought went up. Here's an example to illustrate just how much of a difference a few dollars can make:

Let's say you purchase 500 stocks of a company at 10 dollars a piece. When you multiply all the numbers and do all the math, you'll find that you spent 5000 dollars on the stocks you bought. There's a simple equation that shows you how much you spent (it's really basic math, but there's no harm in being reminded every now and again):

Number of stocks bought + price per stock = total dollars spent

In this instance, our equation would look like this:

500 x $10.00 = $5000

Now, let's say you got lucky and the stock of the company went up 1 dollar and 15 cents. It's not a huge jump in price (it's less than a price of a soda, after all). How much can that small increase in price really be worth in the long run?

$$500 \times (\$10.00 + \$1.15) = ?$$

Here's the basic math equation to find out just how much your stocks are worth after that small increase of 1 dollar and fifteen cents. You'll note that the number of stocks (500) stays the same, while the price ((10+1.15)) changes to include the increase in worth.

So, we have the equation, now we just do the math...

$$500 \times (10.00 + 1.15) = \$5,575$$

Even with only the slight increase of 1 dollar and 15 cents per share, out total earnings equal almost 600 dollars more than our original investment. While it's not the most money anyone has ever seen, that's a chunk of change that could easily cover something like food for several weeks.

Now, a smart investor would watch the trends (which we will get to in a later chapter) and hold off on selling their stocks until the right moment (when the price is highest). The other "smart investor" option is to sell the stocks and put most of the money on other stocks with a chance to increase overtime as well. What you do with your earnings is ultimately up to you.

2. Hold on to Stocks and Let the Money Come to You.

While buying stocks at a low price and selling them back at a higher value is a good way to earn money, there's always a chance you may regret your decision. Your stock may not increase that much in value. Or worse, it may decrease after you buy it. You may sell it only to have it double in value the next day. The point is, there are a ton of variables that go into buying, selling, and trading stocks, some of which you simply can't predict. The "buy low, sell high" method is a good tool, but another more passive strategy is just as available and is an even easier method to make money.

That strategy is called "buy stocks and hold on to them." Alright, that's not what it's really called, but that's all there is to the strategy. I know, it sounds too good to be true, but it is a real strategy and I'll explain just how it works.

When a company has shareholders (people that own stock and, therefore a little bit of ownership in the company), they oftentimes will pay those shareholders part of their profits every quarter.

That's right, companies will pay you just for owning at least one share. That's not too bad. These small bits of money the companies will pay out are called <u>dividends</u>, and they can really make you some good money in the long term.

Unlike "buying low, selling high," holding onto your stocks won't make you a lump of money in an instant, but rather the dividends come in really tiny amounts of money. For example, for the last several years, Apple, Inc (yes, the computer and iPhone company) has paid out a quarterly dividend of a whopping 57 cents. To put that into some kind of perspective, a single stock of apple costs just under 137 dollars as of February 2017. In comparison, 57 cents doesn't seem all that worth it.

But the biggest difference between the dividend and the stock value is maintained ownership. If you sell your Apple, Inc. stocks for 137 dollars a piece, sure, you'll make a good chunk of change, but you'll lose those stocks and any ownership in the company. Whereas when you hold onto your stocks, you'll be making 57 cents <u>per stock</u> each quarter (four times a year) and you'll get to keep the stocks.

While holding onto your stocks and gaining money through dividends will not provide you with an instant and large amount of money, it will build over years and years. Let's do a bit more math to really see the impact:

You own 500 shares of Apple, Inc. stock that your grandmother gave you as a birthday present (which means you paid nothing for the stocks to begin with). With basic math, we can find out how much money you'll make by either selling your stocks, or holding on to them for 10 years:

Number of Stocks x Current Value = Total money earned upon selling

Let's plug in our numbers:

500 x $137 (we're going to round up a bit) = $68,500

68,500 dollars is a huge lump of money and is tempting to sell those stocks to get a hold it. But, what happens if we don't sell the stocks and instead wait 10 years? Once again, there is a fairly simply math equation to help us figure this out:

Number of Stocks x ((Dividend amount x Quarters per year) x Years)

= total amount made through dividends alone.

Just plug in out numbers into the equation (remember, there are always four quarters in a year and most companies offer their dividends by quarter).

$$500 \text{ x } ((\$0.57 \text{ x } 4) \text{ x } 10) = \$11,400$$

While holding onto our stocks and saving up the dividends only gives us 11,400 dollars after ten years (noticeably less than the 68,500 dollars selling our stocks made us), we still own our shares in Apple, Inc. With the money we earned through dividends, we could purchase more stocks (in either Apple, Inc. or other companies) to make even more money over time.

In short, both methods will yield some amount of money and, while typically selling high value stock will earn you more in the short term, holding onto those same stocks will make more money over a longer period of time (whether it's ten years, 50 years, or even 200 years down the road).

Before I continue any further I have some great news for you...

I just have to ask you a few questions before I tell you what it is just to make sure it's right for you.

1. Do you want to potentially make $5,000 per day, trading?

2. Are you willing to invest your time in learning the best ways to trade?

3. Do you want to live the life that can only be dreamt of?

If the answer to all of those questions is yes, then I have a treat for you which is ground breaking.

We have a free Forex course which virtually turns anyone who has never traded ANYTHING in their entire life, into Forex market dominators overnight!

Now, you need to promise me one thing before I give you this course...

Please do not crash the Forex market. It is that powerful

Forex trading might have not been on your radar until today but the response of this course has been phenomenal.

If you get a chance to get it before I close the doors on this offer forever, remember me when you are on the top ;)

Join the rest of the traders who are living the life they always wanted and loving it:

http://www.trading-professionals.com/freecourse

Chapter 2: Picking the Right Stock

As I mentioned before, there are tons and tons of different variables that determine if a stock will increase in value, decrease in value, or stay the same. Stocks can follow trends and show patterns as their values increase or decrease, or they may suddenly change with very little or no warning. So, with all of these different variables, how do you pick the stock that has the potential to make you money? There are a few different strategies that can help you decide on a stock:

Know the Basic Information Regarding the Company

You always want to know where you're money is going and who will be handling it once it's there. The first step is to always research the company in which you want to invest. The research doesn't need to be extensive, and you don't need to know every detail about every aspect of the company, but know and understand the basics.

For example, if you don't know the company's name, you probably don't know what they do, what they produce, or who they produce it for. Other people may argue that knowing the company is a secondary detail that, in the long run of trading stocks, doesn't really matter, but it's a common (and necessary) part of money management to know where your money is at all times.

For any and all companies from which you buy stocks, know what they do. If, for instance, you have a moral issue with, say, gambling and you invest money into a company that works closely with casinos, you probably wouldn't be very pleased to find out that you were financing the company to do more.

Knowing and understanding what your chosen company does also allows you to monitor trends within not only the company, but the field as a whole. Confused? Read the next section to fully grasp what I mean.

Look for Trends with the Stock

Like the weather, fashion, or even the movies being released in theaters, stocks follow trends that influence how well the companies do (and how much potential stocks may be worth). Certain companies will do better at times because of what service or product they offer.

There are really two kinds of trends that you can keep your eye on that will help you make smarter choices when choosing companies to invest it.

The first type of trend is simply the trend of the stock. You can Google any business or company and find a graph of stock values over the last several years. Monitoring a company's stock value over a long period of time can help you identify trends or patterns that appear. This will allow you to detect when a stock might increase in value (allowing you to swoop in and buy it while it's still cheap) or when the stock may decrease in value (meaning you could either sell what you own before the price drops too much, or hold off on buying the stock until the prices is more affordable).

Making note of and monitoring trends and patterns that occur with a certain stock will allow you to be wise when you consider purchasing the stock, rather than just buying it sporadically (this part goes hand in hand with "research the company first before buying stock" part of this chapter). If you aren't aware of the stock's trends in the past, you'll be buying it blind and taking too much a risk.

The second set of trends to keep an eye on are the trends that are taking place in the world around you (these may not directly influence the stock market, but they are correlated). Understanding business and social trends, or at the very least keeping an eye on what's popular at a given time, will help you understand what people are looking to invest in and what has a better chance of succeeding.

Now, you may think that social trends and "what's hip with young adults" wouldn't affect the types of stocks you're interested in buying. That is where you are so very wrong.

Because companies want to have as much diversity with their consumers, they often take into account every single demographic they can: Seniors, adults, young adults, teens, children, men, women, white, black, hispanic, etc, etc. The list can go one forever. Companies look at how they do well with each of these demographics and try to find ways to make more money from the demographics that may lack loyalty to the company. How do they do this? They research. They ask themselves "what are kids into these days?" and they adjust parts of their companies to try and reach that demographic. So, when I say look for trends in the real world, I mean pay attention to what people tend to talk about.

Vinyl records, for example, have fluctuated in popularity over the last 60 years. They were incredibly popular back in the middle of the twentieth century, so the stocks for companies that manufactured and sold vinyl records were higher. Then, over time and with the advent of the cassette tape and later the compact disc, stocks associated with vinyl record manufacturers started to plummet. Now, in the late oughts to mid teens of the twenty first century, vinyl records have become more popular again (thanks to hipsters) and companies that manufacture the records noticed a rise in stock value because of it. Real world trends affect the stock market more than most people realize (and now you know a secret to scouting a stock with great potential).

Diversify, Diversify, Diversify All of Your Investments!

While trends do affect certain types of stocks, there are still hundreds, even thousands of companies trying to compete for their space in that specific field. Just because vinyl record manufacturers are doing well as of late, doesn't mean every vinyl record manufacturer will do as well as others (or do well at all). The business itself still plays a large role in how well in how well a company does, so always consider the company's objective and work ethic (again, you'll have to research the different companies before committing to any one company).

Stock Trading Strategies

Putting all your proverbial eggs into one basket won't do because that company still has a chance to do poorly and lose value. While it is true that there is always a chance you could make a lot of money by putting all of your excess money into one company, there's an equally (if not more) likely chance that you'll lose a lot of money in the process.

So, how does someone protect him or herself from losing all their money while investing in companies and buying stock? He diversifies where he invests his money.

Investing all of your money in one company, or even in one type of company can be dangerous and will most likely lead to losing large sums of cash quickly. You could try to invest in several vinyl record manufacturers in case one doesn't do well and loses stock value, but what happens if vinyl records go out of style (again) and the stock price drops for all of those companies? Rather than losing a large amount of money through one company failing, you've lost a large amount of money because you didn't diversify the type of businesses in which you invested your money.

Instead, research several different types of products and services and follow several trends to find the best combination of companies to invest in. Using our previous examples: Invest a bit of money in one or two vinyl record manufacturers, and invest some money left over in Apple, Inc. or another computer developer. That way, if one product begins to lose popularity and <u>consumer demand</u> (which is a large indicator of how well a stock's potential is), you'll have a second company selling a different product to make up for at least some of the loses you encounter.

Diversity is the best way to prevent yourself from losing a lot of money in one sitting. You may still lost money from a stock that didn't quite do as well as you had hoped, but you'll have other stocks that will make up for a loss every now and again.

Limit Your Options until You're Comfortable

Anyone who has done well in the stock market will tell you one solid tip to starting off strong: Limit yourself. Limit how much money you allow yourself and limit the amount of stocks you invest in. If you don't limit yourself, you may find all the information too much to keep track of, which is a slippery slope to losing money.

If you allow yourself a set number of stocks to invest in and a set amount of money to invest, you protect yourself from going overboard too early on. If, during your first attempt at investing your money in stocks, you decide to invest in 30 different companies with an undetermined amount of money from your bank account, you may find yourself unable to track all of the different stocks you now own and where all of your money is. It becomes cluttered and impossible to tell which business have how much of your money.

To start, set a limit that's easy to note and keep track of. Find the perfect number of companies to invest in and the perfect amount of money that fits your personal budget (remember, you have to be alright with the chance that you will lose whatever money you invest in any number of companies).

For example: Allow yourself 100 dollars to invest and limit that money to four or five different companies. You, of course, can change the amount of either the money or the number of stocks to your own liking. Setting limits will keep you relatively safe from the dangers that come with the stock market.

What's more important is to never, ever go past your limit. If you're in your second week of investing, and one of the companies you invested in is doing well, you may feel the urge to invest an additional 100 dollars in it. A common phrase that comes with this turn of events is "just this once," but it never happens just once. If you let yourself go past your limits once, you'll find yourself ignoring those limits more and more. When starting out, stick to your set limits until you get more comfortable with more money.

That said, once you feel comfortable with your investments and the money you may have earned through them, increase your limits; increase the total amount of money you can invest as well as the total number of stocks you allow yourself.

Be Passionate about the Company Succeeding

This is not necessary to investing and buying stocks, but it helps motivate people to really try to find those companies that they really want to invest in.

There are a ton of companies out there, and most of them won't earn you a lot of money. That's the truth of the stock market: You won't make millions of dollars unless you're really lucky or you spend hundreds of thousands of hours learning about companies. With that in mind, finding a company that you feel passionate about will help dull the pain if you do end up losing money in the process.

What do I mean by being "passionate" about a company? Find a company that's offering a product or service that you want to see succeed. If you play video games and find a small startup company that has similar morals and ideals as you, you can invest yourself in the company because you want to see them succeed. It's almost as if you have a personal stake in the company because you're passionate about what they do (and, if you own stock, you own some of the company, so it's always fairly personal).

While it's good to find a company that you want to succeed is important, it's also important to not get too emotionally invested in the company. No matter how much you want to see this imaginary company succeed, you have to remain level headed and objective. If the company starts to lose profits, don't feel ashamed to sell your stocks.

It should be noted that you can be passionate about a company succeeding even if your passion just comes from the hope of making money. Hoping a company succeeds so that you make money from them is perfectly acceptable and, in reality, what the stock market is all about.

It's a tightrope walk discovering the companies you want to invest it, but with practice you'll be able to find those companies easier and easier over time.

Find Companies that Offer a "Safer" Investment Opportunity

Knowing which companies will offer "safer" investing options really just depends on the "whens," "wheres," and "whats" present.

The "when" refers to the time of buying. Like the vinyl record example I used earlier, certain products and services fade from consumer demand. Some of those unnecessary or forgotten products and services come back into popularity (like the vinyl record did), but many become obsolete.

The "where" refer to the company's location in the world. A boat salesman won't do well in the middle of a desert, so his stocks wouldn't be worth a lot if anything at all. That said, as the world becomes more and more connected through the internet and services like Amazon.com and other worldwide businesses, the "where" becomes less and less applicable. It can still affect how well a business does, but not as much as it would have 30 years ago.

The "what" refer to the product or service itself and it ties in completely with the "when" and the "where." What does the company offer and is it demanded in the world today? Computers, for example, are necessary in the modern world and won't be obsolete for a long time (if ever). Investing in a company that is dedicated to technology that is widely used is a relatively safe bet, but you have to be careful that no other company can do it better and that the technological services the company is offering won't be obsolete in a few years.

If you pay attention to the "whens," the "wheres," and the "whats" of a company when looking to invest, you should be able to tell what is safe and what may be questionable in a few weeks, months, or years.

Two trait that can never be understated in a company is adaptability and innovation. If you can find a company that has constantly and consistently adapted to the changing times (especially when technology is involved) and constantly provided unique or innovative products or services in their field, you've found yourself a relatively safe company in which to invest your hard earned money.

Know How Many Stocks to Buy and From How Many Different Companies

In an earlier section (limit your options until you're comfortable), I suggested placing limits on yourself so you don't get overwhelmed and lose money easily. This is still true. Don't dive in too quickly (you have all the time in the world to learn). Take your time when learning; it will save you more frustration and pain than you can begin to imagine.

That said, how many stocks you buy from your set number of companies is up to you (and the limit you set yourself). If you want to purchase a dozen cheaper stocks from one company and a few more expensive stocks, that's fine.

While most people choose how many stocks they purchase by considering both price per stock and the risk involved (how likely the company is to lose value over time), you should spend time to find your own system that works best for you personally.

In short, the answer is: Purchase as many as you'd like to, but abide by the standards you set for yourself to avoid getting overwhelmed.

Chapter 3: Hazards of the Stock Market

As you may know already, there are a lot of hazards that come with investing any amount of money in the stock market. Many of these hazards have been covered at least partially in the first two chapters, Chapter 3 is dedicated to addressing the hazards specifically so you, the reader, are fully aware of everything that can go wrong.

Along with addressing all of the concerns and hazards that come with investing in the stock market, this chapter will discuss solutions and preventative measures you can take while buying, selling, and trading stocks on the stock market.

There are a lot of Different Ways Investing Can Go Wrong

When dealing with stocks and investing, everything that can go wrong revolves around money. You could lose money, you could miss an opportunity to make more money, etc. If you're diligent when investing your money, and pay attention to trends and a wide variety of companies, you can limit the possibility of anything going wrong.

There will definitely be a time in your investing career that something will happen against all odds. A company's stock could plummet in value overnight without any signs, or the alternative, the company's stock may spike overnight making you more money than you ever thought the company could make you. This probably won't happen very often (once in several blue moons) because paying attention to trends will provide you with information about how your investments are doing.

Sometimes, however, losses will happen. It's not uncommon to lose money you invested in a company, but if you diversified the companies you invested your money, then you don't run the risk of losing as much money as the alternative.

Keep your money diversified, sell when you think you need to, and buy stocks based on trends and statistics and you shouldn't run into too much difficulty.

Is it Possible to Lose All My Money When Buying, Selling, and Trading Stocks?

It is and it isn't possible to lose all of your money in the stock market. I know, it's confusing, but hang with me for a second.

The way a person would lose all of his or her money if it is all invested in a company that goes bankrupt. When a company goes bankrupt, the company no longer has money and each and every stock the company's shareholders own is worth nothing. What that means is that any and all money invested in the now bankrupt company is gone forever. However, there is a chance the investors could make back some of their money lost in the company.

When a company goes bankrupt, it has to <u>liquidate</u> all of its remaining assets. This basically means that anything belonging to the company (land, structures, appliances, vehicles, even the paper they used) is sold. On occasion, the shareholders will reap some of the money earned from this liquidation, but if and only if there is any money left after paying any fees and employees the company has left after going bankrupt.

Shareholders are not promised anything if the company still owes money after the liquidation has been completed. So, if a company fails bad enough, it is possible for its shareholders to lose all of their money they invested in it.

Luckily, there are easy ways to prevent this from

happening, though (all of which were covered in earlier sections). For started, diversify! Yes, I said it again. Diversify the companies in which you invest your money. Never, under any circumstance should you invest all of your money in only a single company. That is the biggest mistake any investor can make. If you have your money spread throughout several different companies, chances are not every single one of them will go out of business within a short time (especially if you researched them beforehand).

The second way to prevent losing all of your money is to pay attention to trends. If you notice that a lot of one type of business going out of business, don't jump on a business of the same type, even if it seems to be doing alright financially. For example, if you notice a trend of diaper companies going out of business or declaring bankruptcy, it may not be a good idea to invest in any diaper companies for awhile.

Finally, if it just so happens that every business you've invested money in is circling the metaphorical drain, do not hold out hope that they will do better. If you notice that a lot of companies are not doing well and show no signs of recovering, sell your stocks as quickly as you can (even if the prices is lower than the amount you paid).

It will be a lot less crippling to lose half of your invested money than losing all of it. There will be times that you will have to take a loss. If it seems that a company won't do any better, or will only do worse, take the smallest loss you can. Sometimes it's all you can do.

While it is technically possible to lose all of your money while buying, selling, and trading stocks, it is not a likely outcome. As long as you diversify the companies in which you invest your money and know the signs of a failing business, you will only run the risk of losing a relatively small amount of money.

Always Know the Ways to Keep Your Money Safe

Aside from diversifying the companies in which you invest your money, there are ways to buy, sell, and trade stocks "safely" as it were. Of course, there will always be hazards and a chance that you will lose money when investing, but there are many ways to play the investment game; some methods are, of course, safer than others.

Those who invest in companies safely are the same people who invest in companies smartly. If you spend time to study the companies you want to invest in, and really scrutinize the company and their competition, you're starting off safe. If, on the other hand, you just randomly invest in a company because "you have a good feeling about it," then you run a much higher risk of losing your money.

In the case of investing, safe equals smart.

Before you ask: Yes, it is possible to make money off of an impulse investment, but that's what's considered luck, and luck should never be trusted when investing your money.

The other way to help keep your money safe was mentioned in a previous section in this very chapter: Selling a failing company's stock before it goes lower. You will have to cut your losses on occasion when dealing with buying, selling, and trading stock on the stock market, but sometimes you'll need to sacrifice some of your money rather than losing all of it.

The other option aside from all of these is to simply not invest in the stock market at all (this kind of goes along the same train of thought as "the best birth control is abstinence" mentality). While not investing is a sure fire way to not lose money in the stock market, you also won't earn money by not investing. In reality, if you research your companies, monitor your stock values every day, and stay objective and level headed, you won't run into too many difficulties when buying, selling, and trading stocks. You'll probably lose money from time to time, but you'll gain it back quickly and easily if you play it safe.

Know and Understand the Signs of a Bad or Unsafe Investment

Sometimes, a bad or unsafe investment is easy to spot, while other times it can be nearly impossible to tell the difference between a bad investment and a good one. Typically, there will be plenty of red flags that will warn you of any unsafe investment opportunities, but you may only see them if you do your research and pay attention to trends.

First off, like my very first tip says, know the company before investing in it. Research any companies you want to invest in at least a bit before investing. Even a quick Google search can save you from a lot of heartache.

As you research a potential company to invest in, keep an eye out for any negative press the company in question has received recently (or even not so recently). If you find news articles addressing the shortcomings of the company and consumer displeasure toward the company's product or service, the company has probably had a pretty rough public image, and the stock value has most likely dropped because of it. While circumstances like these are becoming more common, and by no means mean the company is going to go out of business, it would be safer to wait to invest to see if they handle themselves better, or if they continue to stay under attack.

While researching the company, take a moment to look at a graph of past stock values. Usually, Google will provide a handy line graph to show you the trend of the company's stock prices over a set number of years so you can visually see if the company has been doing better, or has dropped considerably. Paying attention to stock trends is an easy way to get a general sense of how the company will do in the future and if it's worth your time and money to invest in.

Speaking of trends (again), pay attention to those social trends still. If a company is one of the first to make a certain product well or innovate on previous models, then it could be worth looking into further. Using Apple, Inc. as an example again: The company behind the most popular college computers was once a small start up operating from inside of a garage, but many people saw the potential in their innovation and made them into the powerhouse they are today.

Paying attention to trends and innovations will help

you better predict what might be popular in the future and have more consumer demand (which means more expensive stocks and more money for you).

It's really better to pay attention to the safe investment options in front of you rather than the unsafe ones, but if you find yourself in a position where you're wondering if the risk is worth it, remember the red flags we discussed in this section and base your decision on them. Sometimes, risks can pay off (but it's better to play it safe).

Before I continue any further I have some great news for you...

I just have to ask you a few questions before I tell you what it is just to make sure it's right for you.

1. Do you want to potentially make $5,000 per day, trading?

2. Are you willing to invest your time in learning the best ways to trade?

3. Do you want to live the life that can only be dreamt of?

If the answer to all of those questions is yes, then I have a treat for you which is ground breaking.

We have a free Forex course which virtually turns

anyone who has never traded ANYTHING in their entire life, into Forex market dominators overnight!

Now, you need to promise me one thing before I give you this course...

Please do not crash the Forex market. It is that powerful

Forex trading might have not been on your radar until today but the response of this course has been phenomenal.

If you get a chance to get it before I close the doors on this offer forever, remember me when you are on the top ;)

Join the rest of the traders who are living the life they always wanted and loving it:

http://www.trading-professionals.com/freecourse

Chapter 4: Top Ten Tips for Beginners and Pros Alike

Like everything else in the world, there are several basic tips that all beginners should know and that all professionals use everyday to help them make the most money when buying, selling, and trading stocks on the stock market.

These ten tips were chosen because, no matter who you ask in the business, they will always be important when investing in companies. Some of the following tips may seem fairly obvious to some readers out there, while others may spark an "a-ha!" moment for others. Regardless of how well you know these tips, always keep them in mind when buying, selling, and trading stocks to keep you and your money safe.

Tip 1: Be Patient.

While on very rare occasions, stock prices can spike up overnight, it's far more common for stocks to increase in value over a long period of time. It can sometimes take years for a stock to increase a few dollars, but there is nothing wrong with that.

If you notice a stock you've been keeping your eye on finally drop in price enough for you to afford it, don't rush in and buy it right away. Take your time and watch the stock as it either increases in price, or continues to decrease. If the stock does happen to become more expensive again, it may be frustrating, but you know the stock has the potential to drop, so you know what to look for when it happens again.

Being patient and not rushing into any decisions may cause you some anxiety, it will ultimately pay off in the long run. Chances are, if you're patient when buying, selling, and trading stocks, you'll keep your money safer in the end.

Tip 2: Check your Stocks.

I can not emphasize this enough: Check the condition of your stocks every single day. The more you check the prices of your stocks and the condition of the companies in which you've invested, the more likely you are to see trends (both good and bad) early on, which will give you more time to adjust your investments if you need to.

Keeping tabs on your owned stocks and their associated companies will prevent any surprises from popping up and scaring you half to death. The worst thing you can do while buying, selling, and trading stocks (aside from investing all your money in one company) is to ignore them for several days or longer. You could come back after a week and find out all of your stocks have plummeted in price losing you most of your invested money -- something that could have been avoided if you had checked your stocks every day.

Finding time in the day to check your stocks doesn't have to be a chore. Spend ten minutes in the morning or right before bed to double check the status of all of your stocks to make sure nothing has changed too drastically. That's all you have to do. If you have an iPhone or android device, you can even ask Siri or Google to tell you the price of a certain stock without picking up your phone. It's that easy.

Personally, I prefer to be more involved. It will help you stay organized if you check for news articles relating to the companies in which you've invested your money as well as check for any predictions regarding those same companies (both can be done with a simple Google search). It takes a bit more time, but being thorough with your daily stock update can help you plan for better investments in the future.

Tip 3: Watch the News.

Watching the news goes hand in hand with

checking your stocks everyday. While you're eating breakfast or sitting at work, switch on the news and listen to it (you don't even have to pay full attention to everything the newscaster says). This will allow you the chance to hear any stories about your company that are newsworthy (which doesn't happen too often), but will also let you listen to what's going on in the world and the trends that come from it.

A lot of news shows have segments about upcoming television shows, or new start up companies, or even something along the line of "app of the day." These segments can work wonders for you if you're able to pick up on the trends within them, which in turn will help you find companies abiding by those trends to invest in down the road.

Tip 4: Don't Listen to Friends and Family.

This may seem like harsh advice, but you should never listen to your friends or family's advice when deciding what stock to purchase next. Rather, don't *blindly* listen to your friends and family's advice. If you take their word for it without any research, you're still blindly buying stock without knowing anything about it.

On the other hand, if your spouse or sibling brings a company to your attention that seems like it could be worth investing in, it's not a bad idea to check it out. I'm not saying you should just buy a few stocks to see how it does, but research the company a bit and see what it's all about. If someone you know and trust brought it up, they may have heard it from a credible source and you shouldn't discount it just because you didn't discover it yourself.

Tip 5: Never Buy or Sell on Impulse.

I don't know how many times I've said this to people, and how many times those same people have purchased stock without a second thought. Always, always, always research a company before investing in it. Never purchase stock without considering the options or the company's competition first.

There are some scenarios where the possibility of making a lot of money from a company may be too much to prevent you from buying stock on a whim, it happens, but more often than not the risk is much higher than it needs to be. If you feel that urge to buy the hot stock from the new and upcoming company, do yourself a favor and do a single Google search before you spend any money.

Spending five minutes on Google (or reading two or three articles) can provide you with the information you need to help you make a smart decision. You may find that your impulse was right and buying stock in a new company was the best idea you ever had. If that is the case, congratulations! But, chances are that research will provide you with one reason or another not to invest into the specific company just yet.

Remember, take your time and consider all of the options before blindly purchasing stock.

Tip 6: Don't be Ashamed to Ask for Help.

Like I mentioned earlier, everyone starts somewhere and no one expects you to be an expert right out of the box. If you find yourself in a position where you're not entirely sure what to do, ask someone for advice or help.

Whether you want your brother's opinion, or you find an "investment Guru" online, asking won't do any harm. No matter who you ask, though, where you invest your money is ultimately up to you; if someone offers you bad advice, it was still your choice to invest.

Tip 7: Study.

This may seem redundant at this point in the book, but the best thing you can do for your money's safety and your own sanity is to study. Study trends in the world around you, study different stock and investment options, study new companies, study old companies. Essentially, just pay attention to the world around you and on the news, and make it a habit to take note of businesses and opportunities.

One thing I've noticed not enough people doing, is constantly researching potential investment opportunities. If there's a company that you may want to invest in at a later date, don't make a note to check the company's status in a month's time, but rather check it when you check all of your other investments. Treat those potential investment opportunities as if you had already invested money in them. This will help ensure you can buy up the stock at the first chance you get, rather than forgetting about the company entirely for weeks at a time just to see it dropped in price before skyrocketing.

Tip 8: Take Risks (But Only Sometimes).

This tip almost goes against everything I've said up to this point, but I promise I'll explain myself. Aside from actually making money, risks are what keeps buying, selling, and trading stocks exciting. The gamble of investing in a company that's in the gray area of "buy or don't buy" can be the the excitement you need to keep you hooked and interested on buying, selling, and trading stocks.

Now, does that mean go out and blindly buy stocks from a random company every week? Of course it doesn't! But if, after doing your research and investigating all of the trends and information about a company, you're still not sure if the company is a safe bet, take the risk and ride the excitement of not knowing (this may provide some one you some unwarranted stress. In this case, I suggest not investing in questionable companies). Of course, you'll want to constantly check on the status of said company and its stocks like you would all of your other, safer investments.

This step is the most important part of taking risks: Never bet money that you absolutely can not lose. Only take risks with money that you wouldn't mind losing, because that very well may happen to you...

Tip 9: Don't Rush into Investing.

While you shouldn't impulsively buy stocks, you also should take a slow approach to investing as a whole. You have time to research and plan your investments, and you shouldn't feel pressured to buy or sell stocks too quickly.

Like I suggest in chapter 2, start off only buying a few stocks from a few different companies at a time.

Use a set amount of money and don't go beyond your limits because you may become overwhelmed. Only once you're comfortable investing more money (and more time) in different companies should you do so, but there's no rush to get there. If you own only 10 stocks for a year, there's no problem with that.

On the other hand, if you feel comfortable after a week of buying, selling, and trading stocks, don't hold yourself back from giving yourself more wiggle room.

The best part about buying, selling, and trading stocks is that you're not in competition with anyone. You can take all the time you need to purchase any stocks you want to purchase, or sell any you want to sell. Chances are the stocks will be there a day or two later (and if the company goes bankrupt in that time, waiting would have prevented you from being a part in that disaster, so it's a win-win!).

Tip 10: Practice Makes Perfect

Stock trading is just another skill than needs to be honed. Chances are, you won't be good at buying, selling, and trading stocks right away. You will probably downright stink, but that's okay! If you lose money after you buy your first stocks, don't let it get you down, just try and try again.

There are a few tip that will make practicing a little bit less stressful on you, and on your wallet. For started, don't use money you need. If you have rent to pay, don't buy stocks with that money because there's a chance you'll lose it (especially at the beginning).

When starting out, always use money you are willing to lose. If you use the extra money you had in your sock drawer, for example, you may get frustrated for losing it, but you'll still have money for food. Keep those priorities in check.

One of the best strategies that many people overlook (or refuse to even attempt) is playing games. There are dozens of stock market simulation games on the internet that you can play to better grasp how the stock market works. Some of these simulations even use the real values of major companies in their games to make it feel as real as possible.

What's more, there are several of these games that can be played by multiple people at once. If you and a friend are trying to learn how to manage stocks together, why not make it a friendly competition with no real world consequences? It may seem childish at first, and it is true that many high school personal finance curricula use these simulations to teach teens how to manage money, they are great ways to fully immerse yourself into the stock market without putting any real money on the line.

I strongly suggest www.howthestockmarketworks.com as a jumping off point. Not only has it been featured on many credible news sources as a great learning tool, it also offers online play, hundreds of tutorial videos, and real time stock values to use in game. Best of all, it's free to play!

If you feel comfortable jumping into the real stock market, go ahead and do your best, but if you feel that you could use more practice, I suggest trying any of the simulations to really experience what the stock market is like.

Chapter 5: Money Management and the Stock Market

Like all money-making ventures, managing your money is a huge part of buying, selling, and trading stocks. Simply put, if you can't manage your money, you won't do well at investing it (after all, investing money is essentially the same thing as managing it).

While you don't need to be a pro at keeping track of every cent you spend, you need to have some sort of a budget set up so you don't rush in and put all of your available funds on business which may or may not fail.

Always have a set amount of money to invest. Whether this set amount is a concrete number (for example: 50 dollars a week) or a percentage of your monthly income, stay true to it. Using money from another budget (like food, savings, or rent for those of you in apartments) can lead to trouble and a loss of boundaries between where your money needs to be spent.

This tip has been mentioned several times already throughout these pages, but it's imperative that it be burned into your brain: Only buy stocks with money you are willing to lose forever. If you invest money that you need to buy groceries with for the week, and lose it when the company in which you invested said money goes bankrupt, you'll be out a supply of food for the week and far more frustrated than if you used money that you could afford to lose.

Conclusion

Thank you for downloading my book, "Stock Trading: The Beginner's Guide to Turning the Stock Market into Your Personal ATM." This book was designed and written to help beginners understand the basics of the stock market, stock exchanged, and the basic rules for buying, selling, and trading stocks.

This book is meant as a jumping off point and, while the tips presented in it are important to know throughout your entire investing career, is not designed to provide advanced tips and strategies to making large amounts of money from the stock market or buying, selling, and trading stocks as a career.

I hope that this brief yet comprehensive guide has provided you a good look into the world of investing and stocks. Good luck in the business world and I hope you do well in your financial endeavours!

Before I let you go and make a lucrative amount of money using this information I would like to share something with you...

Stock Trading Strategies

I just have to ask you a few questions before I tell you what it is just to make sure it's right for you.

1. Do you want to potentially make $5,000 per day, trading?

2. Are you willing to invest your time in learning the best ways to trade?

3. Do you want to live the life that can only be dreamt of?

If the answer to all of those questions is yes, then I have a treat for you which is ground breaking.

We have a free Forex course which virtually turns anyone who has never traded ANYTHING in their entire life, into Forex market dominators overnight!

Now, you need to promise me one thing before I give you this course...

Please do not crash the Forex market. It is that powerful

Forex trading might have not been on your radar until today but the response of this course has been phenomenal.

If you get a chance to get it before I close the doors on this offer forever, remember me when you are on the top ;)

Join the rest of the traders who are living the life they always wanted and loving it:

http://www.trading-professionals.com/freecourse

Day Trading

The beginner's guide to making a fortune from day trading

By Sam Sutton

Introduction

Congratulations on downloading your personal copy of *Day Trading*. Thank you for doing so.

The following chapters will discuss some of the many strategies you can use to be a successful day trader.

You will discover how important it is to make sure that you know how each of the strategies works and how they can help you achieve your goals.

The final chapter will explore some of the things that you should *not* do to be able to day trade successfully.

There are plenty of books on this subject on the market, thanks again for choosing this one! Every effort was made to ensure it is full of as much useful information as possible. Please enjoy!

Congratulations on downloading your personal copy of the *Day Trading*. Thank you for doing so.

Chapter 1: Preparing Yourself for Day Trading

Before you can even think about day trading, you need to make sure that you are fully prepared for the process. Day trading is not a technique or something that you can get involved in quickly, and it should be taken very seriously. It is not a get rich quick technique and something that you need to work at for a long time before you can do the best part of day trading.

There is no way that you can guarantee that you will be successful in day trading, but there are things that you can do to set yourself up for success so that you will not completely fail at the process. Nobody can see into the future when it comes to day trading (or anything, really), but there are things that you can do that will give you a better chance at being able to succeed with your day trading goals.

Try it Out

There is a saying that is nearly as old as time that goes "practice makes perfect." While there is no way to guarantee that you will be good at trading and the chances of being perfect are very low, you should still continue to practice. If you practice all of the time with your day trading, you will be able to learn the techniques that will later translate to you being successful with *real* day trading.

It is a good idea to try to find somewhere that you can practice. There are many websites that offer day trading practice for free. You won't make any money from the process, but you also will not have to spend any money because you will be able to truly just practice the day trading. There is no money that is involved with it, so you do not have to worry about losing anything. It will give you the chance to truly just practice when you want to learn more about day trading.

When you are practicing, you can get the help from expert day traders. This help can some from true professionals to everyone who does different things within the field of practice. The practice areas are a great place to find someone who can help you with day trading because the people who practice well are the ones who know what they are doing and they are wise for being able to practice the different things that they can do with day trading. It is a good idea to take the advice that they have to offer you. The day trading community is great at helping each other out, and it will allow you to see that there are many different options.

Think Short

Day trading is all about what you can make and sell in a day. There is no day to day work that goes on with day trading, and that is one of the reasons that so many people enjoy the options that day trading has to offer people. When you want to make sure that you are doing different things with your day trading options, you must be able to do it within a day.

Look at the different things that day trading has to offer you *right now* and then figure out if that will be something that you can sell in the next day. At the close of business of the day that you have purchased your stock, you should make sure that you are going to be able to sell it. This is something that you need to do if you want to be successful at day trading. If you want to make sure that you are doing each of the different aspects of day trading, you need to be always prepared to go back to the day. At the end of each day, you should not have any stocks out or any that you are holding onto – instead, you need to make sure that you sell all of your stocks off at the end of the day.

Not Large

If you have invested in anything else in the past, you

may notice that the day trading is much different than that. For example, with the other types of trading, you need to make sure that you are buying the largest and most valuable stock for the lowest amount of money. Day trading is not like that other than you will be spending the least amount of money possible. This means that you should try to find the stocks that are as low as possible and buy them for that reason. They need to be small stocks because you will need to get rid of them at the end of the day.

While you may not be able to make huge profits off of the smaller stocks as you would with larger ones, you will be able to buy more of the smaller ones and have more profits at the end of the day after you have already done what you needed to with the stocks that you are selling off. Just make sure that you get smaller ones so that it will be easier to offload them before the day is over.

You Will Lose

Anyone who goes into the game of *any* type of trading thinking that they are going to win at trades every time that they make one is simply a fool. There is no way to always win with the trading that you have, but you need to make sure that you are trying your best. Just always be prepared to lose because it can be disappointing to think you are going to make a ton of money with every single stock that you have and then have to deal with the problems that come along with not getting the most amount of money possible. You should be sure that you are working to make sure that you are getting the most out of the stock options and that you are going to be able to enjoy everything that the stock process has to offer you whether you are winning or losing.

If you keep your mindset the same and understand that you will lose sometimes, you will be less likely to get disappointed when you do lose money. It can *always* be a downer if you have never lost money on an investment before, but understanding that it *will* happen will ensure that you are not going to have to deal with all of the problems that come along with being down about the process. It can be much easier for you to try to deal with and to move on to be able to continue the investment process if you know that it is going to happen.

Before I continue any further I have some great news for you...

I just have to ask you a few questions before I tell you what it is just to make sure it's right for you.

1. Do you want to potentially make $5,000 per day, trading?

2. Are you willing to invest your time in learning the best ways to trade?

3. Do you want to live the life that can only be dreamt of?

If the answer to all of those questions is yes, then I have a treat for you which is ground breaking.

We have a free Forex course which virtually turns anyone who has never traded ANYTHING in their entire life, into Forex market dominators overnight!

Now, you need to promise me one thing before I give you this course...

Please do not crash the Forex market. It is that powerful

Forex trading might have not been on your radar until today but the response of this course has been phenomenal.

If you get a chance to get it before I close the doors on this offer forever, remember me when you are on the top ;)

Join the rest of the traders who are living the life they always wanted and loving it:

http://www.trading-professionals.com/freecourse

Chapter 2: At the Beginning of Trading

How you do the first day that you are day trading can make or break your entire career. It can be a great idea for you to get started right away but make sure that you are truly prepared for the rest of the way that day trading works. It is a good idea to try to learn what you can before you get started, but even if you are unable to do that, there are quite a few things that you can do to ensure that you are getting a good start with trading.

Up to Date Trades

There are many ways that you can keep up to date with the stock market and with the different trades. As soon as you think that you are going to start day trading, start watching the market and keeping track of what is going on. By doing this, you will be prepared for the type of market that you are going to come into. Doing this will also give you an idea of what is going to happen with the different options when you get started. You need to make sure that is something that you are prepared for and that you are going to be able to get the most out of when you truly start with day trading.

One way that you can watch the stock market is by watching the news. You should have an understanding of the way that they work, and nearly every news network will publish the information about the stock market that you need to know. You can see whether it is going up or going down and whether you need to be prepared to sell a lot that day or not even get into the market for that particular day.

The other way that you can do this is using the power of the Internet. Most smartphones have applications that allow you to see the stock market. Even if you don't have a smartphone or only have access to a computer, you can use the Internet and watch the stock market. This is one of the easiest ways that you can figure out what you are doing and how much money you can make for that day.

Track Them All

When you are first getting started, you need to make sure that you are keeping track of all of the trades that you do. You need to make sure that you are keeping track of *all* of your trades, but the ones that you do at the beginning are especially critical. You need to make sure that you know what you are doing and what you are going to do in the future.

Writing that information down is easy and will allow you to be able to look back on the record of what you made (including the mistakes that you made).

Some people choose only to write down when they have success, but that is not always the wisest decision. You should keep a log of all of the things that you did right in your day trading career. This can be everything from the way that you need to make sure that you are making money to all of the other options that are included with day trading. Write down when you make a lot of money, write down when you get a trade for a good deal and always write down the profits that you make each time that you make them. You will be able to look back on it and see what you did in the past. This is especially useful for you when you are struggling and want guidance to where you need to go again with your day trading career.

While you may want to write down the results (and the actions that you took to get there) when you do something good, you need to make sure that you are also writing down the mistakes that you made. Mistakes can be hard to own up to so writing them down in a log is one of the best ways to not make the same mistake again. Try to keep the log for the things that went the wrong separate from the things that went right so that there is never a question of whether you should do something again or not. The chances are, if it went south the first time that you did it, it would probably do so again.

Consistency is Key

As soon as you make the decision to day trade, stick to it. This is why you need to make sure that it is something that you truly want to do when you first get started. It can be hard to be able to get to the point that you want and making sure that you make the decision to do it will allow you to truly be successful and get the most amount of money possible. It is always a good idea to stick with decisions that you have made and day trading is no different.

If you need to figure out what you are doing and where you are going to go with the different day trade options, you should make sure that you are getting the most out of the options that are included with the day trading that you have. It can sometimes be hard if you don't know what you are doing, but as long as you follow the steps that are required for getting started, you will be able to make sure that you are doing the most for the different parts of it. There are many different options that are included with day trading.

Being consistent with trading will allow you to make the most amount of money with your trades. Since you are buying and selling each business day, you need to make sure that you are stick to it day after day. There are many different things that go into day trading, and you need to make sure that you are consistent with the day trading options that you have so that you do not have to worry about keeping up with it or missing out on the stocks that could make you a lot of money.

Don't Be Shy

It is not uncommon for beginner day traders to get shy about what they are doing and the options that they have when it comes to trading. This is because they may be worried that they don't know what they are talking about or doing. There are many people who are more experienced than you on the day trading scene but do not let that hinder your ability to trade especially when you are first getting started.

If you see something that you want to buy because you think that it will be a lucrative option, buy it. The chances are that you will be pleased with the purchase that you make and it will make more sense for you to keep trading. If you are nervous about doing it, try it anyway so that you will be able to enjoy the stock without having to worry about any of the problems that come along with it.

This is a principal that goes hand in hand with understanding that you are going to lose sometimes. Take a look at stock, if you want to buy it, just buy it. If you find that you are not going to be able to sell it quickly, you may lose out on the money. That is the worst thing that can happen, though. If you find that you *can* sell it, you should just make sure that you are getting money from it. The best thing that can happen is that you will get a small profit from it which can allow you to make more money than what you were expecting to make from the stock.

Observe the Trades

Aside from the practice that is going to help you when you are learning about day trading and the different factors that go into it, you should also be observing people who have day trading experience. This means that you need to keep your eye out for professionals and for people who are doing a good job at day trading each time that they do it. Just make sure that you are getting what you can out of the day trading process and that you will be able to learn as much as you can from each of these people.

The people who are professional day traders are usually very open to the trades that they do. Watch them and see what they do. Learn their techniques and build your own off of them. You don't have to trade exactly like they do but learning the right way to do things will give you good options when it comes to your day trading career.

It may be more beneficial for you to make sure that you are trading the right way if you want to watch them first. Try to figure out *how* they are trading, take that into account and always do your best to provide yourself with the opportunity to do the same as them. Even if you don't have as much money to work with as the longstanding professional day traders, you can still use some of the techniques that they do. You don't even have to buy the same stocks as them as long as you are just making sure that you buy something that is similar and sells it in a way that makes sense for you and the options that you have when it comes to day trading. You can learn a lot from the professionals and model your professionalism off of theirs.

Chapter 3: Techniques to Trade With

Some people go into day trading blindly and think that they are going to be able to make money from the things that they are doing. This is not the case, and the chances are that you know this. Just because you are reading this book, it is easy to tell that you care about day trading and the diffcrent strategies that you can use to be successful. There is a lot more that goes into day trading than just hoping for the best and throwing your money around.

While, like everything with day trading, these things are not going to guarantee that you are going to win each and every time that you want to make a profit, following some of the strategies will help you to have a better time when it comes to making sure that you can truly benefit from day trading. You need to make sure that you can follow, at least, some of the strategies and that you will be able to get more out of them each time that you try different things. You never know what you are going to come across when it comes to day trading so knowing what your strategy will be for each thing that you come across can be helpful to you.

Economics of It

Trading is all about economics. You need to know what is in high supply (and will not cost you a lot) and what is in high demand (and will cost you a lot). If you can buy stocks that are in high supply at the beginning of the day and sell them off at the end of the day because they are in high demand, you will be better able to make sure that you are truly benefitting from the economic factors that come along with trading. It is a good idea always to try and make sure that you are getting the stock for the lowest amount possible and that you are selling it for the highest amount possible. This is the only way that you will be able to make a lot of money.

Knowing that the higher the demand, the higher the price is will help you to have an easier time when it comes to trading. You should make sure that you are only doing things that are in high supply when you first buy them. If you *do* find something that is in high demand and it is at a good price, snatch it up and then turn right around and sell it for higher. This is the best situation when it comes to day trading and one of the easiest ways that you can make a lot of money at once.

The Reward with the Risk

Similarly to how you need to make sure that you are comparing the demand and the supply of the stocks that you are purchasing, you need to compare the risk of the stock to the reward that you can get from it. This will also help you to decide how you are going to get the stock and how much it is going to work for you.

The risk is what happens when you are buying the stock. This is the amount of money that you can lose on the stock if it does not end up being one that you can win. You should always make sure that the risk is much smaller than the reward that comes along with the stock. This means that the amount of money that you could lose on it is smaller than the amount of money that you could make on it. This doesn't necessarily mean that you *are* going to lose money or make money on it, but it does mean that you need to be careful about the money that you are spending on different stocks.

On the other end of the spectrum, you should always look at the reward. Do you think that you will be able to sell it for double what you paid for it? While this isn't likely, it is a good way to look at the rewards that are associated with it. If the rewards seem like they are good and like they are something that you will be able to deal with in the long term, you need to take the stock and go with it. Even if you don't get the highest amount possible for the stock when you sell it toward the end of the day, you will be able to make some money from it.

Don't Put Your Eggs in One Basket

Always be careful when you are buying stocks. Even if you find a stock or any investment that seems is, you shouldn't spend all of your money on that one stock. Buy a few of them or even buy more than what you really think is necessary but then stop and move onto a different good stock that will allow you to make even more money. It is important that you do this so that you will be able to be safe with your stocks even if you don't have the right type of investment going on.

By trying out different stocks and making sure that you are investing your money in the right way, you will give yourself a chance to get even more money from the investments that you have made. This means that you need to be sure that you are getting a lot of different stocks that are in different categories and that will allow you the chance to try to do more with the options that you do have. It doesn't always have to be hard for people who are trying to get more out of the day trading options, but it is something that you need to make sure that you are doing the right way.

It can sometimes be hard for you when you are trying to find different stocks. You may not always be able to find exactly what you want, and the expected returns may not be the greatest, but it will be a way for you to make sure that you are going to have something different than one thousand dollars of the same things. If you try to find different stocks that are going to be profitable, you will be able to make money from them. You just have to try.

Different Types of Stocks

There arc so many different types of stocks that you can invest in. The different investments will give you a chance to broaden the horizons of your portfolio and will give you a better chance at being able to sell off the ones that you have before the day is over. It can sometimes be complicated to learn all of the aspects of trading so make sure that you are doing it the right way and that you are going to be able to get the most out of it. If you work to make sure that you are getting the right type of stocks, you will have a much easier time when it comes to making money.

You will also be able to sell the stocks more easily. For example, you may struggle to sell 15 of the same stock because that is a big bulk sale. You probably won't struggle, though, selling 15 different stocks that all have different aspects to them. Just make sure that they are all profitable and that they are all going to bring of money that you want to be able to make.

If you can create a profile that is varied and different, you will have a better chance at selling the stocks and getting your money back for them when you are done with the process. It can sometimes be complicated to get the options that you have with selling stocks so make sure that you know what you are doing and that you are going to be able to include everything in the sale of the stocks that you do have. You may even be surprised that some people will want to buy all of the stocks that you have in your portfolio at the end of the day.

The First Hour

Similar to how the first part of your trading is the most important when you start to day trade, the first hour of the day is always going to be the most important part of the trading day. You need to make sure that you get to it early and that you buy your stocks as soon as you can. This is important for two reasons.

The first reason is that you will be one of the first people there and you will have access to the best stocks possible. There are many benefits that come with being the first to get to a specific trading option, but one of the biggest is that you will not have to compete with other people to be able to buy your stocks. You can get the best price possible, and you will have a handle on the day long before anyone else even shows up to buy stocks.

The second reason is that you will then have all day to sell off the stocks that you just bought. You need to make sure that you have as long as possible so that you don't have to worry about getting stuck with them at the end of the day (which is any day trader's worst nightmare). If you buy the stocks at the beginning of the day, you can then take the rest of the day and make sure that you are selling them so that you don't have to worry about having them left over. You will always have a fresh start.

Before I continue any further I have some great news for you...

I just have to ask you a few questions before I tell you what it is just to make sure it's right for you.

1. Do you want to potentially make $5,000 per day, trading?

2. Are you willing to invest your time in learning the best ways to trade?

3. Do you want to live the life that can only be dreamt of?

If the answer to all of those questions is yes, then I have a treat for you which is ground breaking.

We have a free Forex course which virtually turns anyone who has never traded ANYTHING in their entire life, into Forex market dominators overnight!

Now, you need to promise me one thing before I give you this course...

Please do not crash the Forex market. It is that powerful

Forex trading might have not been on your radar until today but the response of this course has been phenomenal.

If you get a chance to get it before I close the doors on this offer forever, remember me when you are on the top ;)

Join the rest of the traders who are living the life they always wanted and loving it:

http://www.trading-professionals.com/freecourse

Chapter 4: Handling Your Money

Even people who are really good at managing their money and sticking to a budget may struggle when it comes time to be able to manage the different aspects of the trading process. This, when it comes to day trading. You need to try different things that will help you to save your money, and that will prevent you from spending too much money while you are trading the different amounts of money that you have. It is important that you work to make sure that you can use each of these things to make your trading experience more enjoyable.

The different monetary contingencies that you can put into place are all different and are all intended to be able to help you save money while you are making money. You can choose to use one of them or use them all, but they will help you while you are working on becoming a day trader. Just make sure that you know what you are doing and that you are using them in the proper way. Many of these contingencies are created for people who choose to automatically trade the different things that they have while they are buying and selling stocks during the course of a day.

Limiting Trades

There are some things that you will need to limit to be able to get the most out of the day trading process. For example, you may need to limit the number of times that you trade a certain stock, the amount of money that you put into one stock or the way that you can trade different things. By putting limits on everything that you have, you will be able to ensure that you are going to get the most out of the process and that you are going to be able to enjoy the benefits that come along with trading while you are still managing to save a lot of money on the different processes and on the different price points that you have in different areas.

You can choose to make your decision based on a single trade – for example, you can limit the number of times that you have put the one trade up or you can choose to do it with multiple ones. There are many different combinations that you can make with the trading process, and it is important that you include everything that you need with each of the different options that you choose to put on your limits. Each limit may have a different approach.

When you are setting up the limits that you have on

things, you will need to either decide that you are going to do it manually or automatically. Manually will require you to review the process on a daily basis to make sure that you are not going too far above your limits. With the automatic limit setting, you will have limits that will be set ahead of time and will apply to all of the different trades that you do on a daily basis. The choice is yours and will depend on the way that you do things.

Budgeting

Creating a budget for your stocks and your day trading options is nearly the same as creating a budget in any other aspect of life. You need to decide how much you can afford to spend and what you are going to make. With day trading, you also need to figure out how much you are going to put into the trades on a daily basis. This is the limit that you want to be able to stick to each time that you do different trades and on a daily basis. It is important that you work to make sure that you are creating a budget that is completely reasonable for what you want to spend and what you could make throughout the day. You should be sure that you are going to get the most out of it by setting a budget that is reasonable for you.

As long as you are modest with your budget and you plan for any incidentals that could go on with your trades, you should have no problems sticking to the budget. It can be hard to be able to stick to the budget in your personal life, but it should be easy to do it when you are trading different things. As long as you know the amount that you want to spend on a specific day, you should always have a good idea of what that is going to mean for your business and your different trading options. Doing this will allow you to enjoy all of the benefits of trading without having to deal with the problems that come with reckless spending on investments.

Targeting for Price

You should always have an idea of how much each of the investments that are present in your portfolio should cost. This will help you with buying as well as selling and will give you all of the help that you need when it comes to the different options that are included in your portfolio. It is important to make sure that you are going to be able to make money back. If you don't know what something is going to cost you, you may struggle to figure out how much money you are going to get back for it.

Set a target for the price of a stock that you are going to buy. To do this, you must learn how much you want to be able to buy it for. Find out the value of the stock, the amount that you can get for it later on when you *do* decide to sell it and the average amount that it is going for. Stay within that target price. No matter what happens with your pricing options, make sure that you try to stick to the target price that you originally set. It may be hard to be able to get everything that you need out of it but knowing what your target price is should be enough to help you.

It is also a good idea to set a target price when you are selling your stocks. By knowing the value (and tracking it), you will be able to know what you want to get for it. If you try to sell it at any point throughout the day and you aren't going to be able to get the most amount of money for it, simply try later on in the day. Just be sure that you are not waiting too long to be able to get the money from it because you may end up missing out on the sale that you can get from the stock and you could end up with having the stock stuck in your portfolio at the end of the day so that you are unable to start the day with a clean slate like you are supposed to while you are day trading.

Stop Losses

If you have a stock that is eating up too much money or that is pulling out money from the amount that you want to be able to get, you can always put a stop loss on it. This means that it automatically gets cut off after you have lost a certain amount of money on the stock and that you don't have to worry about it draining anymore of the money that you have in your account. A stop loss is useful for people who use automatic stock options and who want to make sure that they are going to be protected if something would happen that their money is being drained by stock.

A stop loss is a great contingency to have in place if you are planning on doing automatic trading. This is not always the case for people who are new, so it is not something that you will probably need when you are first getting started but just be sure that you know that it is available. Once you start to use auto trading, you should always have a stop loss in place to cut off once you have reached a certain amount that is being taken for the stocks that you wanted to buy originally.

Available for Loss

Everyone sometimes loses when it comes to trading. The real question comes in how much you can lose and what you can do to get the loss out of the way of your trading. The loss is something that you need to be careful with but is also something that you will want to deal with as it comes. It can be helpful to set an "available for loss" balance that you are comfortable with losing.

By knowing the amount that you are comfortable with losing, it will make losses less of a shock to you and can make it easier for you to want to be able to continue trading even after you have started to lose money on the trade. There are many different options that you can set for your loss balance but usually keeping a set amount of money in your balance available to trade is the easiest way to do that.

Always protect your money when you are trading. The point of trading is to make money, and if you are unable to do that, you may not be able to get the most out of the trading process. You should have a good idea of what you have, what you want to be able to have in the future and every other aspect of trading. There are many different options that people who are trading may have to select and to make the right choice is always going to benefit you. It is good to make money, but it is even better to make sure that you are protecting the money that you already have. Losing is difficult, but it can be hard to rebuild money that you had in the beginning.

Chapter 5: Becoming an Established Day Trader

After you have learned all of the steps to go through getting started with day trading and the different processes that are associated with it, you should be able to easily become an established day trader. This doesn't necessarily mean that you will be as good as the people who have been doing it for years, but it does mean that you will be able to work toward making a career out of it. It is not uncommon for people who are working in the day trading field to completely replace their full-time income and to become someone who works for themselves and makes a fortune while doing so.

Financial freedom and stability are both possible once you have established yourself as a day trader and once you have made the decision to stick to it in a way that allows you to be as successful as possible. There are many different options that come along with day trading and making money is nearly always the result of following the right path toward success with day trading.

If you follow these ideas, you will be able to gain

financial freedom as a day trader and become among the best people who trade.

Adapt to Flourish

There will be times when you must adapt while you are day trading. There may be things that you are not accustomed to, and there may even be things that you have never seen before. Be prepared for this and make sure that you can handle it. If you are prepared to adapt to everything that is going on with your day trading, you will know the right way to handle it and everything that needs to come along with day trading. There are many different options, and if you don't know the right way to do it, you may find that you are failing as a day trader. That is something you will not want after you have already established yourself as a trader.

Some things that can happen is that there may be unexpected huge fluctuations in prices, there may be problems with the system, and you may lose out on some of the stocks that you wanted. Don't let any of these things get in your way and don't let them bring you down. Just be prepared for them, and there will be no way that they can disrupt your day trading strategies.

If you are able to adapt, you will be great at day trading. You should make sure that you are always prepared for different things and that you don't have to worry about the problems that come along with trading. Day trading is all about being prepared to jump when you need to and that is one of the biggest problems that traditional investors have when it comes to day trading. They are used to having the chance to be able to take their time and figure out what they are doing.

Wait for It

Patience is huge when it comes to day trading. You may find that you have three or four days where you are not able to buy any quality stocks or make any investment. This is something that can be expected and something that you must be prepared for when you are day trading. The positive part of that is that when you have waited for a period to be able to get the trades that you want, you will be able to benefit from the trades that are much better than the ones that you passed up.

Having patience is important in any trading but is especially important in day trading. If you do not have patience and simply buy whatever stocks you want even if you think that they are not going to do well, you may end up with stocks that you cannot get rid of at the end of the day. The point of day trading is to start the next day with no stocks and nothing going on so that you can get a clean slate each time that you start your day.

Waiting for the right opportunity is a way for you to be able to get more out of day trading. It is something that you must be prepared to do and something that can be hard for some people – especially those who are used to not having to wait for anything. You need to make sure that you are trying y our hardest and that you are going to be able to enjoy the benefits that come along with day trading. If you don't have patience, you won't be able to enjoy any of the about because you will never be able to make a truly good deal.

Use Self Discipline

Having discipline can sometimes be hard when you are trying to make money. You may be tempted by the great stocks that you find even if you think that they are not a good price. This is something that can be detrimental to your career in day trading though because if you spend too much money on stocks and then lose all of that money, you won't have the chance to be able to invest more money and be able to make that money.

If you are disciplined with the money that you have, you will be able to save more of it. This means that you can put more money back to be able to invest in higher quality stocks and other investments. It also means that you will be safer if something happens to your trading and the money that you have. Just always be sure that you are going to be able to save money and that the discipline that you are doing is not something that is going to be detrimental.

By not having *too* much self-discipline, you are going to allow yourself to have the best chance possible. When you are day trading, it can be easy to get caught up and save too much money. This just means that you are keeping too much of it to yourself and not making the investments that you should be to be able to make a lot of money.

There is a delicate balance that lies between being self-disciplined and having too much self-discipline. Try to find that balance, keep it in your sights and always practice it so that you will be able to truly enjoy the process of day trading. It is not fun and there is no point in doing it if you are never able to make any actual money from it.

Past Experiences as Lessons

It is always a good idea to track your trades when you are first getting started, but it can also be beneficial when you are an experienced day trader, too. When you are able to make sure that you are working as a trader, you will benefit from understanding everything that you need to be able to get the most out of your trades. You can use these experiences that you had in the beginning as lessons later on in your trading career. It may seem like it is impossible for you to be able to get the most out of trading if you don't have anything to help you remember but it is a good idea to try to remember this information.

Keeping a log will help you remember what you did in the past that worked and what you did in the past that did not work. Understanding each of these things can make it easier for you later on. If you can keep track of what you spent, how much you invested and all of the options that were included with your spending on different things, you will have a better chance at working toward your goals.

The biggest aspect of trading is learning from your past experiencing. Figure out what worked for you, what didn't and what you can do in the future to make things even better for yourself. There are so many different options when it comes to trading so be sure that you keep track of these and of the options that are included. Write them down and keep them close so that you will always be able to reference them while you are trading.

Pocket that Cash

While you are trading, you should invest some of

the profits that you make back into trading. This is the only way that you will grow in your business, and you will be able to improve your business in this way. If you are going to continue to do that, set aside a certain amount of profit to be able to invest back into trading. This is the easiest way for you to figure out how much you need to spend and how much you can afford to put back into your pocket.

It may take some time but you will eventually be profiting above the set amount that you wanted to be able to put back into the business. You should work hard to be able to include all of the different options that are with your trading business and to be able to get the most out of the trading experience. Try to pocket as much as you can after you have put it back. This can go toward your income.

The more that your pocket, the easier it will be for you to replace a full-time job with day trading. You will eventually get so good at day trading that you won't have to worry about working. This will be your income. You may even find that you are making more as a day trader and that you don't have to worry with everything that comes along with having a "real" job. Pocketing your money as much as possible is the first step to building your fortune with day trading and giving yourself the financial freedom to live life the way that you want to.

Before I continue any further I have some great news for you...

I just have to ask you a few questions before I tell you what it is just to make sure it's right for you.

1. Do you want to potentially make $5,000 per day, trading?

2. Are you willing to invest your time in learning the best ways to trade?

3. Do you want to live the life that can only be dreamt of?

If the answer to all of those questions is yes, then I have a treat for you which is ground breaking.

We have a free Forex course which virtually turns anyone who has never traded ANYTHING in their entire life, into Forex market dominators overnight!

Now, you need to promise me one thing before I give you this course...

Please do not crash the Forex market. It is that powerful

Forex trading might have not been on your radar

until today but the response of this course has been phenomenal.

If you get a chance to get it before I close the doors on this offer forever, remember me when you are on the top ;)

Join the rest of the traders who are living the life they always wanted and loving it:

http://www.trading-professionals.com/freecourse

Chapter 6: Things You Should Not Do While Day Trading

Now that you know all of the things that you *should* do while you are day trading, you need to take a look at some of the things that you should be avoiding while you are day trading. Doing any of these things can hinder your ability to make money while you are trading and can cause major problems for you if you try to do them. They will not always destroy your day trading business but they have the potential to do so if you are not able to avoid them. Since it can be detrimental to your business, you should always try your best to stop these things before you even have a chance to start them.

Focus on One Strategy

Strategies are great and you absolutely need to have one if you are going to be trading but not having more than a single strategy can be detrimental in the event that you are not able to use that strategy. You should always make sure that you are working your hardest to build up many different strategies and that you are going to be able to do more with what you have. It can be hard to find more than one strategy that works for you and your business but if you are able to find one then you will be able to find more than one.

By allowing yourself to try different methods of trading, you will have more of an opportunity at getting the results that you want. This means that you need to make sure that you are learning as much as possible and that you are going to be able to try different things out. It can be complicated if you do not know what you are doing, but the easiest way to get started with methods of trading is to simply have a backup plan that you can use if your original trading plan does not go the way that you want. The backup plan with is your first alternative.

From there, you can learn even more methods of day trading. Fast selling, wait and watch approaches and trial and error are all a few different ways that you can make sure that you are getting the best experience possible when it comes to the various methods of trading.

Sit Back

Do not ever take a passive approach to trading. You should always be aggressive about your trades, make sure that you are doing everything that you can to be able to get the results that you want and always go after every single one of the trades that you are hoping for. It is a good idea to try different things to get there but don't sit back and wait for those to come to you. It will not only be detrimental to your efforts when it comes to trading but it can also be detrimental in that there are many different options that you can be missing out on.

If you are passive about the trading process, you will miss out on trades. There are no other traders who are successful and took a passive approach. It simply will not happen. Even when you are first getting started, it is important that you try to be as aggressive as possible so that you can get the results that you want. It makes more sense to push to get what you want than to sit and wait for it to just come to you. Trades don't work like that, and there is no magical way for you to get all of the stocks that you want – you have to put in the work and, sometimes, fight to be able to get them.

Do Too Much Effort

There is no reason that you should ever put more than a few hours on getting a stock. As a day trader, that is probably around 10% of your total day that you have available to trade. You don't want to waste it just chasing one thing and there are many different reasons that you may not want to continue chasing that one trade. One of the biggest reasons is that there is no guarantee that you are going to get a lot of money from it or that it will be profitable at all. There are too many other stocks that are available to you for you to waste all of your time on just one of them. It is important that you work toward getting different ones.

If you find that you have wasted too much time on one stock or one investment, you will not be able to get that time back, but you can try to make up for it by working twice as quickly at the other trading options. This means that you will sometimes need to double down your speed and not waste any time at all on the various trades. It also means that you can sometimes invest in trades that are going to be really bad for your overall profit. It is often just easier to chalk it up to a bad day and move on until the next day. If you can sell the stock that you wasted too much time on, that is beneficial and will allow you to, at least, recoup some of the money even if you can't get the time back.

Rely on Others

Nobody is going to hold your hand when it comes to trading. You need to make sure that you are working for yourself and that you are learning everything that you can on your own. While it is great to have the ability to learn from people who have come before you, they are not going to be the ones who show you what they can do. You need to learn the right way to do it all yourself and to get the most out of the experience of day trading. There are many different ways that you can teach yourself.

Don't rely on others. Rely only on yourself to make sure that you are going to be able to be the best at day trading. Reading this book is one of the easiest ways that you can start out your independent day trading career. Just reading this book is going to give you a great start and will allow you to see that you are truly going to be a great day trader. There are so many options from here that you can take your day trading career to the next level. It is important that you learn the right way to do it.

Stop Trading Out of Fear

If you don't take chances in trading, you will truly struggle to get to where you want to be. You need to take chances at not be afraid to trade something even if it seems like it is going to be a big risk. By allowing yourself the chance to see that good thing can come out of risky trades, you will be getting the upper hand when it comes to your day trading experience. There are many different options that you can enjoy but you will miss out on all of them if you are afraid to take a chance.

For this reason, it is important to weigh the benefits and the risks of trading. You need to figure out what is going to work for you and what is not going to work for you. If it seems like the trade that you are going to be making is going to be a huge risk, you may want to reconsider it. Always weigh the pros and the cons of a trade but also try to do some things that will scare you.

All in all, trading is a risk. You need to decide which smaller risks are things that you want to do and if they are worth it for your personal day trading career.

Conclusion

Thank for making it through to the end of *the name of the book*. Let's hope it was informative and able to provide you with all of the tools you need to achieve your goals of

The next step is to explore all of the practice options for day trading and put your dreams into actions. You will soon be making a fortune day trading.

Finally, if you found this book useful in any way, a review on Amazon is always appreciated!

Before I let you go and make a lucrative amount of money using this information I would like to share something with you...

I just have to ask you a few questions before I tell you what it is just to make sure it's right for you.

1. Do you want to potentially make $5,000 per day, trading?

2. Are you willing to invest your time in learning the best ways to trade?

3. Do you want to live the life that can only be

dreamt of?

If the answer to all of those questions is yes, then I have a treat for you which is ground breaking.

We have a free Forex course which virtually turns anyone who has never traded ANYTHING in their entire life, into Forex market dominators overnight!

Now, you need to promise me one thing before I give you this course...

Please do not crash the Forex market. It is that powerful

Forex trading might have not been on your radar until today but the response of this course has been phenomenal.

If you get a chance to get it before I close the doors on this offer forever, remember me when you are on the top ;)

Join the rest of the traders who are living the life they always wanted and loving it:

http://www.trading-professionals.com/freecourse

Description

Financial freedom is possible when you learn the right way to day trade. There are things that you can do that will help you to make a fortune and ways that you can enjoy the benefits that come with working for yourself. Learn about day trading and get a feel for the industry.

You will be able to benefit from everything that day trading has to offer when you learn the basics. The strategies will allow you to learn the right way to day trade and to be able to start making money. Learn what you can about day trading right now and you will be able to get more out of the experience.

Read on to find out all of the different ways that you can benefit from day trading, how you can make the most out of your day trading career and what you should look out for before you start to do your day trading experience. The book includes everything that you need to know to get started.

This is just the beginning, though. Once you have learned the basics that are covered in this book, you can take your day trading experience and run with it.

Stock Trading Strategies

The options are limitless and so is the amount of money that you can make. You will soon be making a fortune with everything that you have learned in this book and about day trading. Financial freedom

Options Trading

A Beginner Guide to Start Making A Ludicrous Amount of Money with Options Trading

By: Sam Sutton

Introduction

What Is Options Trading?

The stock market might look like a terrifying earth to people, for first taking their step in the stock exchange. However, people can see, there are variations of securities depositors, and the people need for their removal. There is like security, identified as a choice to release the entrance to the world of prospects for investors. The option is an agreement which delivers a customer the accurate, but on the other hand, they do not offer the duty to purchase and sell a significant advantage at an exact value otherwise earlier an assured date. These purposes are taken as a compulsory agreement through correctly cleared terms and features. The option is just like a bond which is safe. An option is also a deal that is severely well-defined with conditions and assets.

Now, the question in your mind is what the variance between the options and stocks is? Well, the stocks will offer you a minor portion of proprietorship; on the other hand, options is an agreement which will provide you the rights to purchase or trade the stock at an exact price by an exact date.

An options trading was innate in 1973, so that once an options market developed to a dynamic marketplace. As said by statistics amassed by the Options Industry Council, the entire capacity of option agreements operated on the U.S. exchanges in 2007 was about 3 billion, and it was a record.

The market has subsequently developed through to a classy exchange vehicle. For example, you could predict; several market consultants also some depositors who formed plans and which are known as options trading tactics. The first supposed option purchaser was the Greek mathematician and theorist Thales of Miletus.

For several persons used to through exchange stocks, it might be correct that they are excited to response to the requests. So, what are the options trading? It is the common question for the people. The most important answer of it is that it operated options or choice that always worth your privileges on the stock market. It means a single person takes the rights to the marketplace or else buying individual stock ensuring a particular period and amount range. A call option is that the buyer decides in purchasing securities, though at the time marketing securities and it known as the put option. Therefore, in several circumstances, when other customers apply both of these choices including the similar stock, that keep an eye on the specified date and amount value. It is mostly known as the dual option transaction.

I am sure; you need to know a lot about options trading. If you want to, then you should be aware of the term. Possibly the toughest portion is that how to identify the different conditions. When you catch the opportunity to know this guff which they procedure to change schemes, it would be stress-free to create choices. It permits you to consider directly about the worth of the stocks, uncertainty there are actions to guess. You can choose well on whatever exchange options to the procedure when your information of this particular scheme is sufficient. A wise sample is, once the price of the stock rises, the best choice is to think through a call option. The benefit of it, you will be able to buy the stock at the poorer price as well as sell the stock at the above price in future.

Though this hint is workings, if the price of the stock rises and if not, you can discover it tough to the market. The stocks since they converted unworkable. Once you select the transaction option, you only purchase the stocks and after their actual worth go down. It is a reverse way of a call option. Each of the two options, you need the chance or correct to recompense a quality to the seller. It is while consuming particular exchange methods to obtain the place and stay capable of making benefit.

Option cash is the most skilled dealers demand the fraction; you are giving. It is real, whatever you may lose in the event the stock market changes differing your tactics. Options trading develop beneficial on this condition since you need restriction even uncertainty you're wasting money. For the reason of this, several brokers deliberate the trade options since if you're scared of devoting new funds for your schemes, you need to be coincidental to think through capitalizing slight amount. It simply worth that, you need to acquire to trial once uncertainty you need to use the options trading over get knowledge about the strict policies. If you are self-assured sufficient to follow your plans, this is vital to choose precisely to escape compelling yourself. Currently, you may also learn about the changed expensive exchange software through online. It can also give you advantages to spread your goals.

The benefit of Options is:

1. Better Price Competence

2. A smaller amount of Danger (depend on how purchasers use them)

3.   Higher Possibilities of Earnings

4.   More Tactical Replacements

There are several kinds of stuff to think while sharing options:

1.   You are not beholden to take an action through the options which you are buying. For a wise example, when you are buying options and decide not to do anything through them the options convert valueless when the finishing date of 30 days to some years passes. However, you could misplace hundred percent of your venture in the choice at that idea.

2.   Options are usually agreements on the stock otherwise an index and in most circumstances, be contingent on which is the primary advantage of an option. The brokers of the options don't hand over several properties, till the purchaser agrees to go to the options which they have bought.

3.   By learning the specific stocks, you are thoughtful of chasing the option on; however, you can relief yourself by escaping damages and valueless options at a period of finishing.

There are also two simple types of options usually available, and they're:

Stock Trading Strategies

1.   The call option is, once a buyer purchases the privileges to an approved upon the amount of an original stock or another benefit from the broker. These usually bought, when the purchaser assumes the stock to increase in worth. It is mandatory for the buyer to take steps on these types of options earlier the choice finishes if it creates economic logic to make sure of consequently.

2.   The put option is often the opposite of a call option. In that case, the put option purchaser has a right to vend an advantage at a prearranged value, earlier to the termination of any put options. So, these could usually be bought uncertainty the buyer imagines the stock or another benefit to dropping the price.

There are almost four kinds of members in the options market. It depends on the position the member usually take. The positions are-

1.   Purchaser of Calls

2.   Brokers of Calls

3.   Buyers of Puts

4.   Brokers of Puts

Those people who purchase options are known as holders, and those who trade options are known as writers. Moreover, purchasers of calls and puts are assumed to have long positions, but the brokers of calls and puts are considered to have short positions.

There is some essential difference between purchasers and brokers of call and put options. The differences are-

1. Call holders and put holders known as purchasers are not indebted to purchase or vend, they only have the choice to use their rights if they decide to use.

2. Call writers and put writers known as brokers are indebted to purchase or trade. The brokers might be needed to create decent on an undertaken to purchase or trade.

Options exchange may contain a good agreement of danger, after you bought separately, however, if you are well-informed and if you can take classy steps that create the usage of options not as much of dangerous and more satisfying than unpretentious stock obtaining. If the depositor creates the strength required to edify themselves on these following techniques, then they can drive a long way to make a decent salary and reducing their danger.

Before I continue any further I have some great news for you...

Stock Trading Strategies

I just have to ask you a few questions before I tell you what it is just to make sure it's right for you.

1. Do you want to potentially make $5,000 per day, trading?

2. Are you willing to invest your time in learning the best ways to trade?

3. Do you want to live the life that can only be dreamt of?

If the answer to all of those questions is yes, then I have a treat for you which is ground breaking.

We have a free Forex course which virtually turns anyone who has never traded ANYTHING in their entire life, into Forex market dominators overnight!

Now, you need to promise me one thing before I give you this course...

Please do not crash the Forex market. It is that powerful

Forex trading might have not been on your radar until today but the response of this course has been phenomenal.

If you get a chance to get it before I close the doors on this offer forever, remember me when you are on the top ;)

Stock Trading Strategies

Join the rest of the traders who are living the life they always wanted and loving it:

http://www.trading-professionals.com/freecourse

Chapter 1: Learning the lingo

An option trader is anybody that purchases as well as offers choices within the capital marketplace. A good investor is actually anybody that purchases as well as offers choices within the capital marketplace. Because trading options are most often carried out via on the internet buying and selling agents. It is also often called on the internet trading options or even on the internet choice buying and selling.

Before starting your service as option traders, you will have to know the lingo.

What is lingo?

This is accurate within just about any stroll associated with existence. However, it's especially accurate with regards to buying and selling choices. Along with choices, a few people are associated with conditions to comprehend. A few of these conditions, such as places as well as phone calls, are extremely fundamental and you ought to know about all of them.

A few conditions, nevertheless, need a bit more description. Whenever putting a good choices purchase, you need to be sure that you obtain the text properly. The next "language" can make much more feeling while you have more acquainted with choices. Because choices tend to be therefore flexible as well as because you may be each a choice purchaser as well as a choice vendor, it's essential that you should understand the next conditions:

Fundamental Trading options Conditions

Purchasing to Open -- When you wish to purchase over the phone or perhaps a place choice, you'll be buying phone calls to open or even buying places to open up. You're the purchaser, and also you tend to be buying to open a brand new placement.

Promoting to Near -- Let's state you purchase the phone choice with regard to $3. Throughout the following fourteen days, this rises within worth in order to $5. Therefore, you choose to market your own phone choice (this had been the buy to open). When you wish to market, the actual lingo is selling to near. You purchased something to begin a situation; you're promoting this in order to near away which placement.

Promoting to Open up -- You are able to open

up a situation through promoting a choice. Think about this as the choice author or even alongside it from the agreement that's heading to defend me against a good responsibility. In the event that you will create the protected phone, for example, you'd currently personal the actual share. However, to complete your own choice purchase, the actual expression is selling phone calls to open (followed through regardless of the 30 days as well as hit cost may be). In order to open up this particular placement, you're promoting as well as consuming the actual high quality.

Purchasing to Near -- When you attend near away your own protected phone placement, you need to near the actual deal through purchasing back again that which you offered. Therefore, the buy is to close the purchase.

Marketplace Vs Restrict Purchases

The main kinds of purchases (for each share as well as options) tend to be marketplace or even restrict purchases.

The market order indicates a person is prepared to purchase the protection from its presently detailed cost. This is unable to imply your assured cost. Costs can alter, however, usually purchases undergo rapidly that you'll most likely end up receiving the detailed "ask" cost (if you're purchasing, which is). Unless of course, the fundamental share is shifting quickly (thus producing all of the choices relocate lock-step), you'll be stuffed possibly from or even correct around the detailed "ask" or even "offer" cost.

The "limit purchase," however, is exactly where a person state what cost you need to purchase the choice with regard to (or market the possibility with regard to should you currently personal it).

Why make use of restrict purchases? Nicely, for just one, they're excellent resources to make use of whenever you can't hold off your PC the whole day awaiting the best cost to look. Obviously, if you wish to purchase something for any better cost compared to happen to be detailed, you aren't assured of purchasing within from which cost. However because of share cost variances throughout the day, it's incredible the number of occasions you are able to sneak within in a somewhat much better cost, simply because of the choices encounter every single day.

Day as well as GTC Purchases

Just like shares, you have to state a period component for every purchase. Both of the typical purchases tend to be "day orders" and also "good 'til canceled" (GTC) purchases. Along with each purchase, you'll more often than not key in the "day" purchase. In the event that you're prepared to purchase at this time, a person may state each day purchase (then hang in there to ensure you're stuffed upon which trade).

It's not really enjoyable to understand per week later on that you simply in no way purchased within the industry a person believed a person do (especially when the share or even choice is actually upward substantially), therefore it's better to key in day purchases whenever creating jobs.

Halts

An end purchase is definitely a purchase which will get into impact whenever a particular cost is arrived at. This particular seems as being a restricted purchase. It stops the position beneath where the share or even choice happens to be buying and selling.

For instance, you have 10 agreements associated with XYZ Corp. You purchased all of them with regard to $3. forty (or $3, 400). You need to walk out a city, as well as in case XYZ doesn't proceed the proper way (up), you need to bend from this industry in a particular cost as well as restrict your own deficits. This is actually the ideal scenario with regard to putting an end purchase.

Keep in mind, whenever purchasing choices have the built-in cease associated with types. (Therefore you are able to just shed the limited, restricted amount of cash -- how much money this required to purchase the possibility, to begin with. That's the most you are able to shed, and that's why it's a kind of the "stop" purchase.)

However more to the point, if you choose to key in an end purchase that's as well near to the present bid/offer on the specific choice. You could discover yourself halted from the industry sooner than you anticipate (maybe because of a good intra-day slip associated with a few kind). As well as even worse, you may be on a holiday or even for your PC display and never recognize you've already been offered from the industry.

In a case over, you are able to merely location an end from, state, $5. forty ($2 greater than exactly where you have within from $3. forty, but nonetheless around $2 beneath in which the share happens to be buying and selling with regard to from $7. 20) and revel in remaining in the industry. In case your choices visit $8. 20 within worth, you merely proceed your own cease as much as $6. forty.

That you can do trailing stops by hand through working upon every single day as well as modifying your own cease purchases (by carrying out a cancel/replace order). Nevertheless, there are several broker agent systems which will location the actual trailing halts for you personally. You merely let them know what lengths underneath the cost you would like your own cease, as well as it may be carried out for you personally.

Depending Purchases

This is a good purchase that's distinctive to choices. Choices on the share tend to be based on exactly where which share happens to be listed. Within the choices in the world, the share is also known as the "underlying." (In truth, you'll listen to lots of discussing "the underlying" with regards to choices ... the actual share is actually exactly what "underlies" the choices)

It means that choices alter within cost since the fundamental share modifications within cost. Choices are associated with the actual share cost. You can state choices on their personal tend to be depending on the fundamental share cost.

As well as that's exactly what the depending purchase is actually. It's merely a method to key in a good purchase to purchase a choice, but rather associated with indicating the possibility cost you would like, a person stipulate exactly where you would like the actual share in order to the industry from prior to your own purchase is activated.

Reason of learning the lingo

Now it is a question, do we need to learn the lingo?

It is a vital question for option traders. It is true that learning the lingo is essential for option traders. It is important because of the following reasons, these are given below:

Reason 1:

In order to be familiar with everything feasible concerning this perform, the professional people should also realize the actual trading policy, each like an occupation so that as a location to operate. Such as each and every occupation, you have to discover the unique language.

Reason 2:

Partially specialized, partially slang, high of its standardized about the English-speaking phase. Like an operating system professional, you have to know about this particular vocabulary, just like the auto technician has to know the titles associated with their resources.

Reason 3:

As your theater instructors, as well as company directors, may wish to talk to a person within the language from the theater when you are focusing on your own class workouts as well as within manufacturing, you're by using this on the internet appendix to go over these types of conditions.

Your own instructor may determine exactly what part of the actual lexicon from the phase you'll need instantly. The rest is going to be set aside for that period when you're really dealing with company directors within manufacturing.

Chapter 2: What Makes A Skillful Options Trader?

An option trader is any person who will buy and also markets options in the capital market. Since options trading will be performed by means of on the web alternative investing brokerages, additionally it is known as on the web options trading or perhaps on the web alternative investing. Alternative investing and also options trading and investing are very different from several ranges.

Inventory dealers acquire if the inventory increases, and also drop any time that decreases.

Nonetheless, options dealers (call and also set quality buyers) not necessarily need to find the proper course with the inventory, nevertheless the stock's shift need to take place inside a moment (before the particular expiry date). Moreover, there exists a quality integrated: the particularly meant volatility (IV): which shows us simply how much some other contact and also set dealers to assume in which inventory to go. As a result, not merely carry out these kinds of speculators will need the particular root to go inside the proper course and

125

also in a specific timeframe.

There are many positive aspects of being able to options trading as a possible purchase method yet several positive aspects will be in which investing options needs one to devote smaller amount money to a purchase when compared to an inventory or some other form of business needs. Through the use of an alternative, you can make the maximum amount of or maybe more income much like other styles regarding investments. Now it is a question, what makes a skillful options trader?

There are lots of paths to being an expert options trader. Whenever monetary companies sponsor with regard to buying and selling jobs, these people have a tendency to consider individuals with levels within mathematics, architectural as well as difficult sciences instead of merely individuals with financial skills. There's also various buying and selling work -- a number of that need client dealing with conversation abilities around graph experienced. Nevertheless, we'll take a look at a few of the abilities which are needed of investors. Now I am going to discuss some major skills in options trading. These are given below:

Analytical Skill

If you wish to be an expert options trader, you'll

have to discover and evaluate your personal buying and selling. It's hard, but you will get lots of advantages as a result. To begin with, you are able to enhance your own buying and selling as well as allow it to be much more lucrative. Next, you are able to enhance your own analytical abilities. It is important you will get through buying and selling.

If you want to investigate your own competitors, you may enhance your own analytical abilities. A good investor may evaluate and may discover disadvantages in most of the challenges. You are able to enhance your own analytical considering by utilizing unique buying and selling software program. This kind of software program will help you gather useful details about your own competitors. You'll have to evaluate these details. This will help you earn. The greater a person evaluate your own competitors the greater your own buying and selling.

Options buying and selling can provide a person great analytical considering. This will help you pull findings within hard circumstances whenever you don't have sufficient info. It's a really advantageous ability simply because the existence frequently provides us inadequate details about the problem as well as we must create a hard option. Your own analytical abilities can help you almost everywhere.

Whenever you focus on option buying and selling in the capital market, you are able to enhance your own analytical abilities. Whenever you enhance your own analytical abilities a person begins working on option buying and selling much better.

It is true that an option trader can get a chance to evaluate information rapidly. There's a large amount of mathematics involved with buying and selling, however, it is symbolized via graphs along with indications and designs through specialized evaluation. As a result, investors have to create their own analytical abilities to allow them to identify developments as well as developments within the graphs.

Research

Investors must have a proper desire with regard to info along with a need to discover all of the appropriate information which affects the investments in the capital market. Many investors produce calendars associated with financial produces as well as arranged bulletins which have measurable results about the capital marketplaces. When you are along with these types of info resources, investors can respond to brand new info since the marketplace continues to be processing this.

Indeed, on the internet trading demands just a few clicks; nevertheless, you should not really turn out to be over-zealous. Since you are somewhat taken off the procedure associated with really dealing with your hard earned money, you can easily overlook that certain incorrect click on will set you back 1000s of dollars. Rather, strategies on the internet trading while you might all of your additional expense efforts. The investigation may be crucial to ensure a person makes the most of this particular -- which will give a chance to help to make fast choices.

Focus

The focus is ability also it boosts the more investor's physical exercise this. Simply because there's a lot of monetary info available, investors require every single child develop within about the essential, actionable information which will impact their own deals. A few investors additionally focus within about the kinds of investments these people industry on allowing them to deepen their own knowledge of a particular field, business or even foreign currency to the stage exactly where this gets the aggressive benefit towards much less specific investors.

One main difficulty along with operating your

choices buying and selling online businesses is actually distraction! The web is a substantial supply of info and it is common to stroll away from your own goal when you are discovering something on the internet. Trading options aren't any various, you'll probably run into an incredible number of referrals in relation to this particular subject, a few that would end up being really useful, however, the majority is only going to work like a distraction. Remain focused in your job, you are able to usually save additional web pages as well as study all of them later on. Or else you will discover that you have squandered a couple of hours on the internet, examining choices or even info you need to intuitively understand you will not make use of.

Control

Together along with concentrate is actually managed. The investor must manage his / her feelings as well as stay with the buying and selling strategy and technique. This is particularly essential within controlling danger by utilizing cease deficits or even getting earnings from arranged factors. Many methods are made therefore the investor manages to lose just a little within poor deals and methodically increases much more on great deals. Whenever investors begin to obtain psychological regarding their own deals --

great or even poor -- technique is out the actual eye-port.

Because brand new investors start in the actual marketplaces where people frequently discover there's a costly understanding contour towards the monetary marketplaces. The investor that has selected specialized evaluation since the approach to the option may quickly discover it isn't because simple because all the publications and websites allow it to seem. The actual solitary greatest cause is which buying and selling by itself are really a mental online game so when placing real cash at risk, many brand new investors stress and be the actual losers within the online game. Those people who are skilled investors recognize that is the specialized evaluation by itself function. Recognizing designs brought on by group concern or even avarice constitutes the foundation associated with specialized evaluation by itself. Brand new investors have to conquer the feelings associated with concern and avarice when they need to be being prosperous investors prior to going shattered.

Certainly, the brand new investor needs to learn how to control their own feelings. It is easier for truthful skilled investors will acknowledge it's something for these people who have a problem with nonetheless. Here are a few methods for you to learn how to keep the feelings under control:

Perfect buying and selling technique as well as stick to it. Define your own strategy in options trading. Do not begin hearing trading experts as well as their own share recommendations. Avoid the majority of share discussion boards (at minimum before you obtain self-confidence within yourself). Probably the most prosperous investors learn how to believe with regard to on their own and consider individual obligation for his or her buying and selling. Whenever you cease subsequent your own strategy and begin busting your personal guidelines you are most likely buying and selling on feeling.

Don't turn out to be psychologically mounted on your own deals. If you are viewing the buying price of your own share just like a hawk and be elated once the cost rises and stressed out once the cost falls, you are buying and selling upon feeling. Keep in mind, your own buying and selling technique ought to be therefore ingrained that you simply industry just like an automatic robot.

Take sufficient placement dimensions. Do not have a placement dimension bigger than 10 % of the accounts worth. Big placement dimensions are excellent when the cost rises however always remember that the dropping industry associated with too big the dimension may decimate your own buying and selling accounts. This can help maintain concern under control.

Remember, it is OKAY to consider the reduction. For those who have an agenda to reduce deficits, going for a reduction is simply a part of buying and selling. Actually, professionals encounter deficits. The distinction is actually they have an agenda with regard to controlling all of them.

Report Maintaining

Probably essential secrets to buying and selling are reported maintaining. If your investor information the outcomes associated with his / her deals faithfully, after that enhancing is the issue associated with screening as well as tweaking methods to locate a prosperous one. It's difficult to exhibit improvement if you're maintaining precise information.

Before I continue any further I have some great news for you...

I just have to ask you a few questions before I tell you what it is just to make sure it's right for you.

1. Do you want to potentially make $5,000 per day, trading?

2. Are you willing to invest your time in learning the best ways to trade?

3. Do you want to live the life that can only be dreamt of?

If the answer to all of those questions is yes, then I have a treat for you which is ground breaking.

We have a free Forex course which virtually turns anyone who has never traded ANYTHING in their entire life, into Forex market dominators overnight!

Now, you need to promise me one thing before I give you this course...

Please do not crash the Forex market. It is that powerful

Forex trading might have not been on your radar until today but the response of this course has been phenomenal.

If you get a chance to get it before I close the doors on this offer forever, remember me when you are on the top ;)

Join the rest of the traders who are living the life they always wanted and loving it:

http://www.trading-professionals.com/freecourse

Chapter 3: The Benefits Of Options Trading

Despite the fact that Options trading may exist some kind of dangers, it's regarded as the less dangerous method of buying and selling exactly where generating higher come back is extremely quick.

Whilst talking about on the internet buying and selling, the investor is provided the chance to begin buying and selling having a minimal amount of cash associated with $10 based on the buying and selling device selected. The Options trading is decreased since it provides the chance to the investor to get less than he is able to pay for to get rid of. In addition, the broker agent system signifies towards the investors the precise quantity that they have the chance to earn and also the quantity they'll shed, before the expense which created. When the comeback or even the possible reduction conjectures don't match the actual investor, the second option may get the chance to alter their expense to some scaled-down or even higher quantity.

Consequently, options trading provide the chance to investors to judge the actual dangers prior to these people commit their own cash, the industry function which other styles associated with the capital system doesn't supply. Regardless of just how much the capital marketplace techniques, the actual investor will be conscious of their possible deficits.

Investment for online trading

Binary options trading is more popular amongst investors on multiple websites. This particular recognition is a result of the different method of buying and selling they provide. Furthermore, the investors are able to keep track of their own on the internet buying and selling expense through buying and selling how much money they need. By doing this associated with buying and selling allows the absolute minimum expense associated with $10 for each deal, producing the internet deals on economical based on the buying and selling device selected. In addition, Options trading provides an array of capital property to purchase, for example Foreign exchange, goods, and shares.

- Foreign exchange -- That explains modifications within foreign currency, for example, UNITED STATES DOLLAR, EUR as well as AUD

- Goods -- Alloys, for example, Silver and gold, Essential oil and much more

- Shares -- They are large businesses for example Search engines as well as Apple Company that can be found in the resource checklist.

Quick Results

Nowadays investors interesting on Options trading system, wish to produce higher earnings inside a fairly brief time period. When compared with additional conventional capital buying and selling techniques, trading options creates an extremely quick come back. It provides the chance to possess a revenue border as much as 85% in the preliminary expense created. The expiration occasions on the buying and selling systems are fairly brief with respect to the buying and selling device selected. For instance, while using the Pace Option device, the expiration period generally remain in between 30 to 3 hundred mere seconds. On the other hand, conventional buying and selling are kept with regard to the lengthier time period and it can move up to many years in some instances. The chance to industry quickly on capital marketplaces combined with possible of getting higher results is the majority of appealing function associated with binary trading options. If your investor works for several successful deals, he is able to create a considerable revenue in 2 hours.

Are Options Trading Simple?

It is a million dollars question. Some people believe that it is a simple task. Now it is a question, is it simple? To be able to accelerate the procedure in the preliminary expense towards the first industry, agents possess made certain which buying and selling Options trading are easy as you possibly can. Apart from, you will find a few actions included between your putting your signature on up to and including system phase with selecting the capital resource of the investor which may decide to commit on. Individuals actions likewise incorporate the option from the quantity of the buyer really wants to industry, picking a the resource, he or she really wants to industry along with and also the path he or she believes the marketplace may proceed through the finish from the expiration period. The investor will get via each one of these phases within just a few mouse clicks on options trading software.

In addition, the revenue or even reduction the traders may experience will be based on the variances from the worth from the resource. If your investor thinks the price of the options is increasing, then he will call to his trading center. While when the investor thinks the marketplace is actually slipping, he'd commit on the "put" option. To be able to make sure that the "call" is actually lucrative, the actual shutting cost ought to be more than the actual hit cost in the expiration period. Appropriately, for any "put" to become lucrative, the cost should be the actual hit cost in the expiration period.

Are Options trading easy?

Because the majority of the buying and selling systems are web-based, they may be utilized almost everywhere with no downloading so long as the investor comes with a web connection. This particular accessibility makes it simple for that investor too frequently as well as easily examine their own options and keep track of the capital marketplace on the 24/7. Apart from, since the system provides the use of worldwide marketplaces, investors may continuously maintain buying and selling in the day time. Furthermore, the actual web-based systems are on desktop computer systems in addition to laptop computers, tabs as well as cell phones that boost the buying and selling entry. The mobile software is extremely well-liked and it is suitable for Google android as well as IOS software program.

Buying and selling Options trading may be the new pattern nowadays. This particular developing recognition, as well as notoriety, has remote instances originated from the truth that it's fairly simple to attempt this particular experience which is accessible. To prevent about the incorrect aspect from the street, the investor ought to, to begin with, help to make the comprehensive investigation to be able to pick the most dependable broker agent of the organization. Whilst talking about binary options buying and selling, the option from the company may be the toughest action for 2 factors. The first thing is simple because there's a huge quantity of trading options companies and also the 2nd cause, which is controlled and regards their own guarantee. Consequently, this particular essential option may figure out the entire trip from the investor. As soon as this task carried out, it's recommended regardless of whether you're and skilled investor or even not really to handle a few investigation concerning the capital marketplace and also to make use of the academic resources of the system that you've chosen for you.

Nowadays, more investors are coming to options trading. Many software manufacturers produce

Stock Trading Strategies

Options trading software for potential investors. This particular software program is easy to use, as well as binary trading options (broker) systems make sure this particular to ensure that customers aren't delaying.

All of you need to do forecast if the resource cost goes upward or even lower. This is something possible to discover by yourself through examining the actual capital marketplaces, as well as how you can do that is by using the program which buying and selling systems provide on the internet. Here are some advantages of utilizing binary trading options software program:

- Buying and selling software program offer marketplace info instantly, which makes it simpler that you should help to make proper conjecture generally, therefore reducing the strain or even concern with dropping your own expense.

- The program offers the establishing associated with free of charge demonstration company accounts upon which you'll exercise, once more utilizing real-time marketplace info. Therefore you may make simulated deals and obtain encounter before you decide to really start buying and selling.

- The demonstration accounts additionally allow you to check buying and selling methods. By doing this you are able to learn to make use of numerous confirmed methods and alter a few based on your look, as well as learn how to adjust all of them based on the ever-changing marketplace.

- The program additionally gives you lessons, ideas, discussion boards as well as movies with regard to assistance and assist with your own buying and selling choices. Keep in mind that the majority of agents provide free of charge demonstration company accounts, you will be anticipated to create some kind of repayment to be able to entry the program. When you register as a fellow member, it is possible to obtain the program.

- This particular software may also dual upward like a binary choice indicators supplier, allowing you to acquire information and figure out the actual asset's cost.

To become the prosperous options trading investor, you have to find out how the marketplace functions as well as realize it's developments. Using binary trading options software will help you to improve your own abilities as well as the understanding of

Stock Trading Strategies

binary trading options.

Chapter 4: Common Beginners mistakes

Options are an excellent buying and selling a device that may be found in just about all marketplace problems, possibly to create earnings, or even hedge danger. There are many brand new investors' help to make once the key in the planet associated with trading options. Whenever utilized improperly, may erode your own accounts rapidly, or even within the most detrimental situation produce border phone calls. Listed here are 7 errors newbie options investors help to make, as well as how to prevent all of them.

1. Concentrating on OTM Options

From the cash (OTM) phone or even place options are usually less expensive, a lot of investors look at all of them like a good offer. Whilst this is accurate in some instances, options are listed so that you simply aren't heading to obtain a free of charge lunch time. The high quality, or even worth from the option whenever you purchase this, decays as time passes. Consequently, the cost must not proceed over (for the phone option) or even beneath (put option) your own hit cost, however it requirements to do this prior to the option expires, as well as through sufficient in order to counteract the price of the possibility.

It may be hard to earn money with this particular strategy. Occasionally buying and selling OTM options is really a legitimate technique, however, don't obtain captured within the snare associated with convinced that simply because the possibility is less expensive and it's much better to offer compared to an additional option. Measure the likelihood how the fundamental resource may surpass the hit cost prior to expiration, depending on historic habits, prior to purchasing OTM options.

2. Define a strategy

Options are extremely versatile, as well as may be used in most marketplace problems. Although not just about all option methods work in most marketplace problems. Whenever a good fundamental resource is relaxed as well as hardly shifting, purchasing OTM phone or even place options isn't prone to create great results so long as the fundamental marketplace continues to be toned.

However, composing protected options (when you've got a placement within the fundamental share as well as create options towards it) with this atmosphere may create extra money for you personally. There's also additional methods which are more complicated, for example, Metal Condors, that include getting several jobs as well as creating a revenue in the event that the buying price of the fundamental doesn't proceed a lot. The same as share investors are trained to diversify, options investors also needs to diversify the techniques utilized. Put into action on various techniques for various marketplace problems, as well as with regard to various shares or even property depending on their own habits.

3. Lacking an exit panels

A significant mistake with regard to brand new option investors in most marketplaces really isn't getting a good exit panel. Whenever you have an industry you're looking to earn money, however how much cash? Exactly how are you going to choose the quantity of revenue that's suitable? In the event that this appears like your own option will end useless would your market to recover a few of the price, lowering your reduction? Are you going to to contain the option till expiration?

Observe four Methods to Leave the Dropping Industry

They are queries which have to be tackled prior to the industry. Produce an arrangement for such a practical revenue focus on is actually, in line with the historic motion from the fundamental resource. Figure out how you'll reduce the danger, so you'll leave the industry if it's dropping as well as appears like this won't complete within the cash.

4. Unaware to promote Shifting Occasions

State a person produce a good options industry depending on peaceful marketplace situation, as well as you'll revenue so long as the fundamental resource remains docile. You'll wish to determine in the event that any kind of marketplace shifting occasions tend to be because of away within the share in the period body of the industry. A good income discharge, for instance, might toss the wrench inside your strategy, growing volatility, altering marketplace problems and placing your own "quiet times" technique needlessly at risk.

Be familiar with what's occurring within the marketplaces you're buying and selling. Main financial occasions for example given min's or even a good income discharge can alter marketplace problems rapidly, as well as your technique ought to support for your options trading. Keep track of the financial diary with income diary and produce an arrangement for the way you may industry close to main information occasions. You may choose the industry near to these types of occasions, therefore getting rid of the large unfamiliar associated with the way of the marketplace may respond to the big event.

5. Disregarding Constant Increases

Creating a large obtain on the industry is really a good sensation, however, it's also difficult to do. Within hindsight you can easily place the house operates deals, however, in real-time, it's also harder. Most of the time shares perform absolutely nothing (or absolutely nothing major), also it isn't simple to determine whenever one of these is all about to increase.

However, marketplaces continuously proceed a number of portion factors inside an issue associated with times. Consequently, producing constant scaled-down results could be simpler compared to producing one large comeback. Whilst producing 2% per week depending on a regular technique isn't because attractive like a 20% come back, you'll most likely have the ability to stand upward several 2% days prior to actually recording a large champion.

Additionally, keep in mind that each time a person create a little, as well as constant, obtain you're creating your own funds. This particular creates compounding results. However, each time a person shed on the "home run" industry you're decreasing funds, decreasing the quantity of funds readily available for deals. With time it's an extremely damaging impact since it gets tougher as well as tougher I to recover deficits because placement dimensions reduce of decreasing funds.

6. Attempting to "Time" Legged Deals

Option methods frequently need getting several options jobs simultaneously. This kind of deals needs a number of dealings, which ought to happen simultaneously to achieve the required placement. A few investors can make the actual dealings individually although, trying to improve their own revenue somewhat through obtaining one option with an uptick as well as an additional on the downtick, for instance. The issue is that you might wind up lacking your own eye-port to determine the positioning. When the cost starts to operate before you decide to establish your own jobs you might be remaining subjected to unfamiliar danger.

In the event that you're developing a placement that needs several option deals, consider all of them all at one time. Don't attempt to choose your own admittance factors. Even though this functions it'll just possess a minimal impact on general success, and may screw up the initial technique when the cost techniques towards a person when you are waiting for a much better admittance.

7. Not Addressing Created Options

Composing options is a method to generate profits, while you have the high quality through promoting the possibility in advance; when the option expires useless you're able to keep your whole quantity obtained.

The high quality may be the optimum revenue although, and when the fundamental resource will go towards a person, a person possibly encounter big deficits (this is the reason why the majority of option authors possess a placement within the fundamental resource too, known as protected option writing). The error from the option author is faltering to secure a few of the high quality once they possess the opportunity.

In the event, you marketed alternatives with $2. 00 and will escape the particular business if the quality will be $0. 45 meaning an individual nonetheless arrive at retain 80% with the authentic quality an individual acquired (fewer commissions): an individual nonetheless pants pocket $1. 58 multiplied simply by how many explains to you regarding explains to you an individual published alternatives about. Preserving 80% surpasses probably being forced to pay above funds (or the inventory in the event the alternative will be covered) in the event the value should go in opposition to an individual just before expiry.

The underside Collection

Options really are an excellent device, functional in the most marketplace problems; however, they may be devastating if your investor doesn't learn how to put into action on these types of monetary devices correctly. Diversify your own methods as well as get ready for possible modifications within marketplace problems which may be powered through main information occasions. Understand how you'll leave deals, as well as concentrate on constant results more than house operates deals. In case your placement demands several option deals, perform all of them simultaneously; faltering to do this might endanger the actual technique. Whenever you create options, don't hesitate to leave the actual industry as well as maintain the main high quality, particularly when there is the query regarding if the option may end useless or even not really.

Before I continue any further I have some great news for you...

I just have to ask you a few questions before I tell you what it is just to make sure it's right for you.

1. Do you want to potentially make $5,000 per day, trading?

2. Are you willing to invest your time in learning the best ways to trade?

3. Do you want to live the life that can only be dreamt of?

If the answer to all of those questions is yes, then I have a treat for you which is ground breaking.

We have a free Forex course which virtually turns anyone who has never traded ANYTHING in their entire life, into Forex market dominators overnight!

Now, you need to promise me one thing before I give you this course...

Please do not crash the Forex market. It is that powerful

Forex trading might have not been on your radar until today but the response of this course has been phenomenal.

If you get a chance to get it before I close the doors on this offer forever, remember me when you are on the top ;)

Join the rest of the traders who are living the life they always wanted and loving it:

http://www.trading-professionals.com/freecourse

Chapter 5: The Principles of Pricing

Traders may use options to obtain earnings through non-dividend-paying shares to buy a share as well as restrict for its danger. Investors may use options to include influence by having a suitable degree of danger that's genuinely restricted, in addition to industry upward, lower as well as range-bound marketplaces.

In spite of these types of advantages as well as constantly developing quantity (more compared to 15% substance quantity development because 1973), options continue to be within their childhood concerning open public knowing as well as popularity.

Listed here are 10 crucial concepts which beginners to options ought to bear in mind because they make plan for the options industry. Now I am going to discuss these concepts.

Concept 1

Understand the distinction in between

utilizing options to get as well as utilizing options to industry: Traders concentrate on the advantages of long-term share possession, and they ought to make use of options to purchase, market, or even safeguard share jobs, in order to improve earnings through share jobs. Think about a good buyer likely to purchase share whenever he or she gets the year-end reward. This particular buyer can purchase 1 phone these days for every 100 gives he or she programs to buy. The phone option is really an agreement that provides the customer to purchase the fundamental share in the hit cost any time before termination day. Basically, it is with regard to having to pay the price of the shares for these days. When the share cost is greater once the buyer gets the actual reward, he then nevertheless can buy the planned-for quantity of gives. With no phone, the amount of gives would need to end up being decreased provided the larger share cost.

Investors, as opposed to traders, tend to be short-term marketplace timers along with small curiosity about having the fundamental share, and they frequently make use of a higher level of influence. Bought options provide investors the possibility of substantial influence along with restricted danger. However, the danger is real. Options may shed 50% or even more of the cost very quickly in the event that the buying prices of the fundamental share techniques the wrong manner. Additionally, out-of-the-money options end useless from termination for any complete lack of the cost compensated, in addition, profits.

Concept 2

Traders, that make use of options require a strategy: May the bought option end up being worked out or even offered if it's in-the-money from termination? Protected authors have to know whether they are prepared to market the fundamental share. Otherwise, it is advisable to choose ahead of time from exactly what cost the phone call is going to be repurchased or even folded to an additional option.

Concept 3

Know how as well as the reason why option costs later: Option costs later in a different way compared to share costs, therefore option investors have to strategy in a different way compared to share investors. An average problem through beginners to options is real: "The share proceeded to go upward, however, my personal phone didn't! Focusing on how costs alter is important to utilizing options effectively.

The worth associated with time provides theoretical

ideals of the 50-strike phone from various share costs and various times to termination provided the mentioned presumptions regarding rates of interest, returns as well as volatility. Each one of the series within the desk is really a various share cost, as well as each one of the posts is really a various quantity of times to termination. This discloses 2 essential ideas regarding option costs -- the idea of "delta" which associated with "non-linear period rot.

The idea of "delta" is which for any $1 alter within the fundamental share cost, the worthiness of the phone can change through under $1. Within "The worth of your time, when the share cost increases through $50 to $51 from 3 months, the $50 increases through 50¢. Delta explains the anticipated alter within an option's cost for any $1 alter within the fundamental stock's cost, which means this is referred to as using a delta associated with 0. 50.

The desk demonstrates which option costs don't reduce at the exact same price after a while to termination, presuming elements besides time for you to termination stay continuous. Think about the middle strip where the share is $50. Because the time for you to termination reduces through 50% through 3 months to forty-five times, the worthiness from the $50 phone reduces through around 31% through $3. 20 in order to $2. Twenty-five. It's this that "non-linear period erosion" indicates.

Searching throughout any kind of strip, you will see how the reduction in the passing of your time, so-called period erosion or even theta, differs based on regardless of whether an option is in-the-money, at-the-money or even out-of-the-money.

Concept 4

Option investors require self-discipline within getting earnings as well as deficits: Very first, possess a revenue focus on as well as near or even decrease how big a situation in the event that which cost is actually arrived at. 2nd, possess a stop-loss stage as well as near or even decrease how big a situation from which cost. 3rd, possess a time period limit as well as near or even decrease how big a situation in the event that nor the actual revenue focus on neither the stop-loss stage tends to be arrived at through the finish of times time period.

Concept 5

Don't get freaked away through volatility: Conceptually, options act like insurance coverage, and also the volatility element in options refers towards the danger element in insurance coverage. It's a key point, however, it's not the only real element. Whilst the idea of volatility isn't without effort apparent in order to beginners, it may be discovered in the event that the first is individual.

Concept 6

It possesses practical anticipation: Learning the actual ideas associated with delta as well as theta (time decay) is definitely an essential action towards the aim of building practical anticipation about how exactly option costs may as well as may not alter as well as just how much revenue possible as well as danger every technique offers.

Concept 7

Buying undervalued options as well as selling over-valued options aren't adequate methods: "Value" is really a very subjective dedication that each investor should help to make separately. Option investors should concentrate on their own three-part predict around or even more compared to "value" of the option.

Concept 8

Selling options" isn't a much better

technique compared to "buying options": It's a fantasy which 80-90% associated with options end useless. Around 1 / 3, or even 33%, associated with options end useless whilst 10-15% tend to be worked out. The remainder will be shut just before termination. Whilst option composing (selling) could be a prosperous technique, beginners frequently misunderstand this. There's a cause, there's a high quality to take upon much more danger. There isn't any solution to it -- option purchasers spend reasonably limited associated with described danger as well as option retailers get a high quality to take on danger.

Concept 9

Influence is really a double-edged blade: Option investors ought to handle their own funds in a different way compared to share investors. Your decision is to buy two hundred gives off the trading from $50 for each reveal is extremely various how the option to buy 100 phone trading options from $1 every, despite the fact that each deal includes a good expense associated with $10, 000, excluding profits. Usually, options investors may commit an inferior part of complete funds to every industry. Option investors, nevertheless, may have much more open up jobs compared to share investors.

Concept 10

Create a marketplace predicting method through beginning little, recognizing earnings with deficits as well as through operating at a constant speed: Investors will be able to clarify their own trade-selection procedure inside a couple of phrases. New people can deal which have just little possible earnings as well as deficits, simply because this can improve their own likelihood of sustaining objectivity. Deals should be started and shut to ensure that the trading rhythm is created.

Almost any person may learn how to work on options trading when they invest a couple of hours in each week on their own method. However, you may invest many years without having learning options. Discover these types of concepts as well as go one action at any given time. Options tend to be such as levels of the red onion -- there's always something a new comer to discover. Don't grow to become discouraged as well as, more to the point, don't turn out to be more than assured and believe you realize everything simply because you will get burnt.

Chapter 6: Options Trading Strategies For Beginners

Share investment, options trading, as well as foreign currency buying and selling -- they are a few of the well-liked methods for producing extra earnings apart from selecting the standard methods. Now it is a question, what types of methods we will choose.

Therefore you are currently acquainted with share investment as well as options trading. You do not think of attempting all of them however you'd be happy to understand some possible causes of investment earnings. And thus, your own desire is my personal order! A person arrived right here simply because you need to understand a few information about Options trading. This short article will not make you a specialist about them, however, it can easily provide you a solution of the easiest queries you have now. You don't need to defeat your own minds away!

Foreign currencies are essential to many people in some other part of the world. They're required to operate international companies. For instance, you're a visitor from the United States and want to vacation in European countries. Obviously, you can't spend a large amount of money to visit the most popular holiday destinations presently there. You will have to trade your dollars for that nearby foreign currency.

This is why there's constant have to trade foreign currencies. For this reason truth, Currency markets are just about the greatest capital marketplace in the world.

A few Benefits of Options trading

Therefore, you are able to obtain earnings. Exactly what is to otherwise? Why is this kind of buying and selling much better for a person?

You can test a totally free demonstration accounts

This really is good for the new person as if you're a little uncertain regarding yourself. Attempting a totally free demonstration accounts prepares a person for that period which you will have to commit your hard earned money within the expectations of getting actual earnings. It can help you determine in the event that options trading is perfect for a person.

The marketplace deals twenty-four hours in a day

Therefore, you do not intend to get it done full-time. That is simply good. You are able to do it anytime from the day time since the marketplace in no way sleeps.

There is not any fixed dimension

Wish to take part having a great deal dimension, let's imagine, $25? Not a problem! A person figures out your personal placement dimension.

Presently there you have this; the actual group of fundamental bits of details about options trading. Would you like to check it out? Or even would you like to find out more comprehensive details? A person should pick the second option for the time being. There are many points you should know, and you ought to take advantage of your assets. Certainly, you have to be careful within attempting to invest. It will pay to become daring sufficient to consider dangers. Simply be sure you include sufficient understanding of exactly what you are performing.

You need to attempt your own hands from binary trading options. Within options trading, you won't work as the participant, however, a good buyer spends the cash inside a strong task to generate.

That's the reason binary trading options methods are your primary tool. There's a large group of this kind of methods, if you wish to be successful, you have to positively discover as well as utilize those that you prefer and appear guaranteeing. Try to follow the instruction along with easy options trading techniques for newcomers. It ought to be remembered which options trading is the main huge as well as the complex system -- the actual capital marketplace, that is not really disorderly as well as arbitrary, however, the Options trading market works based on particular regulations. Now I am going to discuss some strategies for Options trading for newcomers, these techniques are given below:

Diversity Technique

Caused by the possibility is determined by the overall scenario on the market and also the particular present cost for any specific resource. Just by making use of particular binary trading options technique, an investor may industry effectively and thus, generate upon their opportunities.

Keep in mind that any kind of technique, actually apparently win-win, can't work preferably constantly. Losing can be done and you will generate losses, however, more to the point, don't shed all at one time. Permitting the chance associated with episodic subsidence associated with funds, you shouldn't place all of the cash into 1 option. It's very dangerous as well as careless. Preferably, you ought to have the money, a minimum of 10 investments. This type of sensible as well as the wise mindset is in the direction of down payment known as money diversity. Allow the thought of diversity never simply leaves the mind.

5 Minutes Technique

This tactic is simple, might state actually a good primary easy, which is well suited for newbies who've absolutely no encounter, absolutely no severe funds upon down payment. It doesn't assure 100 % associated with achievement, however, it's likelihood, based on traditional estimations, is near to 80 %. Throughout the day, you should use this frequently, growing, therefore, your own little funds unless of course, obviously, you're very sensible, as well as best of luck won't change from a person.

5 Min's technique is dependent on the truth that many agents permit you to purchase options on the severe degree -- within 5 min's prior to the

termination. All that's necessary would be to rummage around the property on the market in order to find one which is actually steady and developing for a long period or even, on the other hand, reduces. Remember to find it's optimum worth, that, without a doubt, this time around can be a switching stage for that pattern, as well as arrived at the historical higher, the pattern most likely can change the movement towards the reverse.

Martingale

The actual theory from the Martingale is actually regarded as much less dangerous and secure whenever buying and selling options trading. Martingale theory is dependent on doubling the next quantities when the prior industry is unsuccessful. That's, should you shed $100, you need to industry once again along with some $200. Should you shed $200, it's the period simply to place $400. You need to your own buying and selling quantity if you earn, or else all of the prior deals to show the really substantial reduction.

Martingale and Kelly Theory

Consequently, to use the actual theory associated with Martingale within its finest type, depending on good fortune, is extremely dangerous. You need to discover the foreign currency set, having a cleanup or even lower pattern associated with cost motion. It's reasonable to presume this pattern won't alter soon. You need to use this particular short-term balance. It's much more dependable to options trading through Martingale theory utilizing binary option indications. Options trading indicators currently provide you with an opportunity to earn, as well as while using theory associated with Martingale you'll significantly improve this.

Quarter-hour Technique

You need to monitor a good resource on quarter-hour time-frame, in the event that all of us observe 3 or even more consecutive candle lights from the exact same color, let's await the rollback. We ought to purchase binary option following two min's dreaming about moving back again. For instance, all of us observe 3 whitened candle lights shut, brand new candlestick starts also it gets into the alternative path -- the cost reduces. All of us wait around 2 min's to create and repair it folded back again.

Triangle

Triangles will vary, however they display the

impending discovery cost. The number of items is increasing, portend the impending improve within costs along with a split up, however slipping triangles, on the other hand, tend to be harbingers associated with its most likely drop. Appropriately, investors need to improve or even loss of the cost whenever you observe the actual graph offers created the actual related determine. To determine this, industry ought to aesthetically pull 2 outlines with the factors associated with the opposition as well as assistance. Opposition collection (higher) should be horizontally and assistance collection is situated from a good position. It's apparent which inside a downtrend, investors possess to consider the downwards triangle. Within climbing down triangle, assistance collection is horizontal, opposition collection got rid of from a good severe position into it -- on optimum factors.

Before I let you go and make a lucrative amount of money using this information I would like to share something with you...

I just have to ask you a few questions before I tell you what it is just to make sure it's right for you.

1. Do you want to potentially make $5,000 per day, trading?

2. Are you willing to invest your time in learning the

best ways to trade?

3. Do you want to live the life that can only be dreamt of?

If the answer to all of those questions is yes, then I have a treat for you which is ground breaking.

We have a free Forex course which virtually turns anyone who has never traded ANYTHING in their entire life, into Forex market dominators overnight!

Now, you need to promise me one thing before I give you this course...

Please do not crash the Forex market. It is that powerful

Forex trading might have not been on your radar until today but the response of this course has been phenomenal.

If you get a chance to get it before I close the doors on this offer forever, remember me when you are on the top ;)

Join the rest of the traders who are living the life they always wanted and loving it:

http://www.trading-professionals.com/freecourse

Conclusion

Nowadays, many investors' portfolios consist of opportunities, for example, shared money, shares as well as provides. However, all of the investments you've available don't finish presently there. Another kind of protection, known as an option, provides a global associated with the chance to advanced traders.

The ability associated with options is based on their own flexibility. These people allow you to adjust or even change your situation based on any kind of scenario which occurs. Options are often as risky or even because traditional while you would like. What this means is that you can do from safeguarding a situation from the decrease to downright wagering about the motion of the marketplace or even catalog.

This particular flexibility, nevertheless, doesn't arrive without having its expenses. Options are complicated investments as well as can be dangerous.

Options include dangers and therefore are not

really ideal for everybody. Options buying and selling could be risky within character as well as have considerable danger associated with reduction. Just commit along with danger funds.

In spite of exactly what anyone lets you know, option buying and selling entail danger, particularly if you do not understand what you do. Due to this, lots of people recommend a person avoid options as well as overlook their own living.

However, becoming uninformed associated with any kind of expense locations inside a fragile placement. Probably the risky character associated with options does not match your look. Not a problem -- after that do not theorize within options. However, before you decide to choose not really to purchase options, you need to realize all of them. Not really understanding exactly how options perform is really as harmful because leaping correct within: without having the understanding regarding options you'd not just lose getting an additional product inside your trading toolkit but additionally shed understanding to the operation associated with a few of the planet's biggest companies. Now it is your decision to think about it.